IoA Institute of Architecture (Ed.)

Aleksandra Belitskaja,
Benjamin James, Shaun McCallum

iheartblob
–
Augmented
Architectural
Objects

A New Visual Language

Birkhäuser
Basel

Obj. 92–182
An Act of
Submission. 100–181

Obj. 183–273
An Act of
Liberation. 182–269

iheartblob – AUGMENTED ARCHITECTURAL OBJECTS:

GERALD BAST

A NEW VISUAL LANGUAGE

"The forms of modern life can be differentiated in various ways, but what ties all of them together is their fragility, temporality, vulnerability, and tendency toward constant change."

Zygmunt Bauman

We live in a world that is characterized by change, insecurity, ambiguity, and an increasingly high degree of complexity. The uncanny and the uncertain are constant companions of our times. The speed of progress in scientific and technological knowledge as well as the increasingly urgent need for solutions in the manifold areas of global challenges — such as: aging societies, climate change, backlash in democracy and human rights, migration, economic inequality and poverty, digitization of human labor, and the preservation of cultural heritage — require radical new forms of education and knowledge acquisition in inter- and cross-disciplinary, synergistic and analytical strategies. Humankind's power to make things happen will no longer express itself so much by putting thoughts into material form, but will instead manifest itself in linking intellectual, intuitive, and social processes.

Investigating new tools, new visual languages, new methods of distribution and new theories is crucial to confront and challenge the intensity of our times — in architecture and beyond. With their interdisciplinary experiments, iheartblob create ephemeral extensions of architectural spaces into virtual dimensions and thus fantastic objects. Their investigational approach founded in theory and criticism kickstarts a much-needed discourse that embraces fragments and complexity instead of shying away from it. Their reflection about a shift in architecture through virtuality leads to a reflection about society and current cultural processes as a whole as well as an observation of 'liquid times' (Bauman), in the truest sense of the word.

♥ : PUT-TING THE HEART IN BLOB

GREG LYNN

In my Angewandte studio we loved the formation of "iheartblob" by Sasha, Ben and Shaun and now that they are graduated it is great to watch where they will go with it. Their work has changed with the times while staying rooted in the recent past, much like a good "alternative" rock band adopts a sound that works and moves it towards contemporary concerns. The idea is right there in the title and it is an idea and a title that I have to say pains me all over again in exactly the way I was pained in the 1990s by fifty percent of their formulation; the blob part, that is. My greatest regret was investing effort in formulating an essay and design method using what was either referred to as 'digital clay' or 'blob' modeling software. I didn't want to confuse geometric principles with clay so I argued for the BLOb (Binary Large Object). It completely backfired and the term was my greatest success in coining a term, but its meaning was not of a new kind of rigor but of an amorphous gelatinous accident. The critical review of which I am proudest summed up the entire blob situation: William Safire's "On Language" essay in the *New York Times Magazine* in 2002 that I will cite with a very long quote as it sheds light on the situation today with Ben, Shaun and Sasha:

"The architect Greg Lynn coined the term blob architecture in 1995 with no derision in mind. He was drawing on a computer, clicking out a random cloud of points that assumed an amorphous shape, loose and formless as an amoeba, which digital designers sometimes call a 'biomorphic form.' Lynn tells me the term 'blob' comes from a sort of acronym for a technical description of a computer-formed shape — a 'binary large object.' Although blob architecture "lacks the elegance, rigor and beauty that comes from modules, proportions and symmetry,"

Lynn says, "in due time, the blob architects

———1
William Safire, "THE WAY WE LIVE NOW 12–01–02: ON LANGUAGE," The New York Times Magazine, Dec. 1, 2002, Section 6, page 42 of the National Edition.

will discover a new form of beauty and elegance in the voluptuous, rhythmic and undulating forms of the differential calculus." The envelope-pushing architect has seen his term shortened to blobitecture. Those planar types who prefer traditional forms like cubes and spheres — and who look askance at the seeming shapelessness of what developed into a new style — seized on the predigital meaning of blob: a bubble or a globule of liquid resembling a teardrop, with an extended meaning of a gooseberry or duck's egg, which cricket players treat as a zero — hence, an error or bonehead play." [1]

The "blob" in iheartblob is not only lacking the elegance, rigor and beauty that comes from modules, proportion and symmetry, it is also intensely reflective, often translucent, always intensely colored, sometimes patterned and occasionally textured. This is what Safire called the "shapelessness of a new style" all over again.

But there is something very different and contemporary that distinguishes their interests from the late 90s, and this is what I find interesting. For me, the sooner the 90s' sloppy blobs are forgotten, the better. What I am most impressed with is the "Heart" of Shaun, Sasha and Ben; that is their commitment to social media, crowdsourcing and what is fundamentally a change in the value of algorithms. In the 90s, there were debates over what algorithms were used and their formal consequences. Friendships were destroyed and civil discourse was abandoned over disagreements about algorithms. The focus was on the medium of architecture and the expert formal use of design algorithms. The algorithm was a code for executing particular shapes, forms and spaces.

With iheartblob, the algorithm is what Google uses to rank results with its search engine, or what Facebook/Instagram uses to determine individuals that look alike others. The "heart" in iheartblob is the new algorithm of what digital marketers call "engagement." In the funnel of the digital with "awareness" at the top of the funnel, followed by "engagement," then "conversion" (otherwise known as a sale) and then "community" or advocacy by customers. iheartblob is one of the first and purest expressions of digital engagement culture framed as a stylistic posture and method of publication. This arc of social media focus has been watched by all of us the last four years. Beginning with algorithmic processes intended to discover happy accidents the three moved quickly to game engines, augmented reality, filters and machine learning.

All of the tools that are the foundation of Snapchat, Facebook, Instagram and Search Engine Optimization they are adopting and using for stylistic effect. I hope you enjoy the book, and if you do, please follow @iheartblob

USER MANUAL

This book consists of a non-linear interwoven investigation into the current state of architecture and technology. Short texts, uncanny imagery and interactive augmented reality content consider the state of architectural discourse at momentary instances through over 250 unique designs. The use of new tools and new visual languages challenge everyday aspects of the discipline, as well as more esoteric notions of architectural theory — its history and the philosophies that shape it. The book itself is an object of experimentation, where its digital companion is waiting to be revealed, where a small vertical line indicates the digital extension of the images. Each object stands on equal ground: each image, each text and each interactive augmentation draws on the tenets of a flattened hierarchy where the investigator is of equal importance within the project.

To experience interactive augmented reality content, download the free app on the App Store or Play Store by scanning the QR code below.

Obj. 1—91
An Act of Rebellion.

Each surreal Architectural Object seeks response from a stagnant architectural discourse. Stemming from pure architectural speculation alongside novel theoretical ideas, ultimately confronting discourse. Typical architectural parameters do not apply – as scale, gravity and inhabitation are discarded, with sensuality, purity of space and form taking their place; theoretical and philosophical thought is intrinsically embedded. Dynamic aesthetics challenge the depths of architectural identity, exposing its limitations as simply a facilitator of space. Instead, space itself becomes the provocation of new approaches in form, technology and discourse.

RIPPED NEAR THE SEAMS

MICHAEL YOUNG

If one can see a seam, one witnesses the fault lines of assembly. A seam is the visual residue of parts, discrete elements, differences, joined into a moment that reveals the artwork as artifice. It is understandable then to realize just how much time artists spend working on seams. They are erased here, added there, subtle in some places, jarring in others. A feeling exists that if there are no seams, then there is something dishonest about the aesthetics of the designed object. Yet rarely do seams map directly from the underlying construction to its surface effects. This applies equally, albeit differently, to images and architecture.

These feelings regarding the perception of the seam stem from cultural lifetimes of aesthetic engagement with art and with the world. They betray assumptions about the ethics of craft and the self-reflexivity of articulating knowledge and skill. Also mixed up in this amalgamation of intuitions, hunches, suspicions and clichés are concerns about realism. But what realism are we talking about? Verisimilitude in naturalist painting? Documentary bluntness in photography? Flatness in collage? Raw materialism in Art Informal? Everyday quotidian events in cinema? Material tectonics in architecture? Low-res pixel glitches in digital imaging? Abstract idealism in philosophy? This list could go on. We would have to agree that there are different "realisms" in each case, but this list only increases confusion. For now we believe that the major decision in defining realism lies with determining the boundaries between mediums, disciplines, and maybe even periods of art practice. If this is the case, we fall either into realism based on a specific medium, or we infinitely regress into a claim that realism is simply a constantly changing subjective assignation. To claim that realism amounts to a direct expression of a medium or to personal whim does not help much in clarifying a definition.

Let us return to the question of the seam, for this seemingly simple instance contains some crucial aspects of our problem. I will specifically look at two kinds of seams; those in built architecture and those in the speculative images that architects produce. If a built piece of architecture appears seamless it produces an aesthetic experience of abstraction; surreal or even unreal. An architecture of the seamless monolith immediately triggers associations beyond the legibility of known construction. It is often deployed to produce exactly this feeling of "How is that built?" It is important to remember that all architecture is made of parts, so if the building appears seamless, it means that the

aesthetics of the surface have been purposefully disturbed to create a different affect. This removal of seams is quite familiar within popular movies as seen in the design of alien spacecraft or other worldly cities as smooth streams of unknown material fantasy.

The counter-proposition is so ingrained in modern architecture that it seems self-evident. If an architecture exposes its construction, its joints, its materiality, it possesses an honesty, a truth, a claim towards realism. This is the case even when the surface cladding has no relation to the structure within. Think of modern architecture's love of exposing the board-formed strips on a monolithic structural material such as reinforced concrete. Architects are much more comfortable with this decorative surface aesthetic than they are with a trowel smooth shotcrete wall. This comfort level has to with an aesthetic of seamed pieces feeling real, while the seamless feels fake, deceptive.

Think about how odd this situation is, for in both cases, the abstract monolith and the highly tectonic construction we are obviously talking about physically existent buildings in the world. They are both "real" in this manner. The difference is aesthetic. The "seamless" desires distance from a standard appearance of an architectural construction, while the "seamed" reassures notions of how an honestly assembled piece of construction should look. Both would thus appear to be invested in an aesthetics of realism, but from opposite positions?

I disagree with this understanding of realism.

I will argue that realism as an aesthetic affect is only produced when there is a tension between an object and its appearance. If an architecture completely disengages from its context (physical and cultural), it positions itself within the realm of fantasy. In its most provocative propositions these are utopian critiques. If an architecture completely engages its material tectonic expression, it positions itself within an adherence to tradition, craft and context. In this instance, the best examples are phenomenologically embedded experiences of place. Neither are what I would claim as an aesthetic of realism.

Realism produces a doubt in sensation. It elicits a second, a third, a fourth glance at the phenomena. It puts pressure on the assumptions regarding how the world appears. There are many conditions where this tension can be created in archi-tecture, but to stay focused on the question of the concealment or revelation of a seam in construction, a much more common word may be used; *decoration*. Decoration, either as uniform whitewashed stucco or as a floral wallpaper pattern, conceals the physical material assembly for an alternate aesthetic character, mood or atmosphere. This is a shifting of one material effect towards a conceptual or sensory affect in tension with what may lie underneath, or even a tension with the visible material itself. All architecture does this in one way or another, as noted above, to either distance the appearance of the architecture from common reality or to embed the architecture more deeply within the material realm. But the issue of decoration is also where we can examine the aesthetics of realism in its most politically provocative manner. An important distinction is that realism is not naturalism. The aesthetics of realism involves an estrangement of the assumptions concerning how reality appears. This estrangement is often produced through the intervention of abstraction. Realism and abstraction within aesthetics should not be viewed as antithetical concepts. If built architecture can disturb scale perception, interior to exterior clarity, relationships to context, understanding of support and supported, material origin, etc. it begins to put pressure on how reality appears. These are very abstract operations, yet they never desire an escape from reality into fantasy, nor do they ever desire an uncritical reaffirmation of values as they are received in a particular place and time. This is a political claim for aesthetics. As Jacques Rancière would put it, aesthetics can produce a redistribution of the sensible.

How do these issues shift when we move from built architecture to the speculative images that architects produce? If the image is seamless it feels real. By this I mean to speak to the veracity of the image itself, not its content. The content can be a fake mermaid, moonwalk, or Loch Ness monster, but if the photographic surface seems unadulterated, whole, mechanically indexed and well, seamless, the photo provokes a feeling of a naturally occurring reality. This question takes on opposing aspects in the case of collage and photomontage. These are artificial assemblies and they typically express their seams. Many of them would fail as artworks if they did not embrace the abstraction of the flat, excised fragment, playing artificially against different photographic contexts. The effect is of clarity and honesty in revealing the photographic medium as one of paper to be cut and recombined. If a photomon-tage is done so well that the different pieces fit together seamlessly, a queasy, uncanny feeling arises. These seamless montages are often derided as lies, as seductions, as fakes pretending to be real, thus suspect in their intentions.

There are obvious parallels and differences here between the aesthetics of realism in built architecture and within the representational speculations that architects produce. As opposed to built construction, the seamless image looks real while the seamed collage looks artificial. This immediately would suggest that realism in image-making is different than in building. But the question is more complex than this, and it is ultimately one of ontology. The seamless image looks real, but is distrusted as actually existing. The assembled image looks fake, but is believed as the constructed representational artifact. This apparent contradiction has to do with an ethics of exposing the medium. There is trust generated in an image that exposes its seams. It creates an awareness in the viewer, a visual knowledge of the abstract nature of its construction, similar to exposing the tectonic joints in a built architecture.

The seamless image has a different affect, one often emphasized in discussions on the digital image. We know that a digital image is an assemblage, a collage of discrete parts, pixels, codes. Yet, the digital image can be manipulated and manifested such that these seams are no longer visible, and this produces the feeling of being lied to. Within many art practices, including architecture, there has been a response in recent years to expose the digital pixel or voxel, to lower the resolution until the abstract chunkiness becomes part of the visible aesthetic. Some of this work has been exquisite and exciting, but in my opinion, not because it exposes the medium of digital images as an aesthetic of realism. A fair amount of low-res art and architecture is a reaction to previous stylizations of digital rendering. I would suggest that there is not that big of a difference between a digital image and a chemical image when it comes to the aesthetics of realism. Both have always manipulated appearances before and after the image is "captured." The more important difference is in how the image is stored, disseminated, and manifested. These differences alter the size and constituency of an audience, and they displace the authority of the institutions that underwrite the legitimacy of the image. These concerns deal with the construction of cultural context and are important when addressing the image culture of our current media-saturated world, especially when considering the ethical and epistemological aspects.

My claim is that the aesthetics of realism is not medium specific. The differences in mediums have more to do with ethical and epistemological differences than aesthetic. When people get upset at a photo-real rendering, it has more to do with the *knowledge* that the image is fake, and the *deception* that the author is trying to conceal it. This is not a question of the aesthetics of realism, it is an argument against the intentions and the actions of a representation that simulates the look of the real. Abstraction is seen as a more truthful mode of representation since it clearly acknowledges the flatness of the image plane and the artifice of construction. But, abstraction works within multiple aesthetic regimes and does not automatically provide any direct access to knowledge just because it may reveal a medium. As said above, the aesthetics of realism are developed through the tensions between an object and its qualities. Within image making, this estrangement can be produced both through concealment of seams and exposure of seams, what matters for realism is that the representation provokes doubt regarding what is represented. If an image can convince the observer that what is represented is real, then make them look closer, pay more attention and suggest that there are significant problems in this reality, then we have an aesthetics of realism. As noted above regarding built architecture, abstraction as an aspect of estrangement can be linked to the effects of realism. An intervention into an image that makes the background look strange or that displaces the obvious use of an object, or questions the relations between foreground and background are all abstract operations found within realism in image-making. Often, these abstractions hinge upon the concealment of certain seams and the revelation of others. Sometimes this is at the level of the medium, sometimes within the scenario depicted. What realism demands is that these abstractions produce a tension, a doubt, a problem with the real as opposed to an escape or a critique.

Architects make images with the desire to effect the real. This aspect is why so much pressure is put on the mediums through which architecture develops it discourse and expresses its intentions. This is also why it is easier and clearer to teach the image-making practices of orthographic drawings. These images are measurable and abstract, they sit clearly in their plane of the page, and often expose the processes of their construction. They provoke the ethical feeling of honesty and express the epistemological aspects of disciplinary knowledge. They are also considered as the loci of translation between design and building. But, there are problems in these assumptions. Outside of the very real technological changes occurring within architecture's representational and construction mediums, the discourse of architectural ideas is also part of the discourse of cultural ideas. To exclude the realm of the photographic image or to regulate it only to the production of critical awareness as disjunctive montage, is to distance architecture from one of the most important developments in the cultural and political aesthetics of the last one hundred years. Architecture ignores these discussions of the image at the risk of its own relevancy. Instead of retreating into an ethics and epistemology of the clearly articulated seam, architecture would do well to look at its own built history and realize that the important questions are not those of being "true" to a medium or a material, but instead are found in those moments when architecture provoked a transformation of assumptions regarding how the real is made sensible. These moments are the prime examples of an aesthetics of realism.

WHY YOU SHOULD CARE ABOUT STYLE

FREDRIK HELLBERG
& LARA LESMES

A LETTER FROM
SPACE
POPULAR

The choppy waters of style are treacherous, yet we navigated them lightly, as one would a ball-pit rather than a daunting ocean.

Understanding style does not rely on having its meaning explained by an expert or historian. Style is recognized intuitively, and produced through repetition. Style is about nodding to each other through our influences, our preferences — and as architects, through our work. Style is not imperative; the strength of any style relies on its ability to communicate.

Trying to claim that a style is one's own is like trying to own a piece of the wind and keep it safely in your pocket. Style can never be about the individual.

Embracing style means abandoning the struggle towards individual genius, innovation, originality; it means dropping the saber and embracing the fact that nothing is created in isolation. Style is about us, about appreciation and exchange.

We cannot name a style as it is forming, but that does not mean we cannot perceive it. In fact, at times it feels like we perceive far too much: we live in saturated times, and it's hard to know which bits of culture will calcify into an enduring style, and which will be discarded. Style needs your attention, because it does not exist unless you see it.

The speed, accessibility and vastness of the Internet has thrown us into a dizzying free fall: our neurons feast and choke on an overdose of pattern recognition. If style is driven by cumulative and collaborative exchange, then the Internet is no less than a style-making paradise.

At the same time, simulated reality is currently undergoing a paradigm shift. Representational media is moving from the visual plane — in front of us — to the experiential sphere around us.
The growing presence of immersive media means that virtual architecture is not only a reality; it is a lucrative and rapidly growing phenomenon. For the first time, instead of being represented by media, today architectural experiences can exist wholly inside it. It is time to review our description of architecture as something only physical.

Comparing the historic evolution of styles and media formats for this exhibition has revealed parallels and correlations too intriguing to ignore. What we have found — and attempt to demonstrate in Freestyle — is a path of continually expanding inclusivity in the production and recognition of style. The ambition of any media is to constantly widen its reach. If style depends on media, then its inevitable goal is to engage more of us and with greater intensity.

We do not attempt predictions about the future of style, or what architecture will look like, but rather how style will reach us and what that implies — that the inclusivity, openness and emancipatory character of new mediums can only be positive for architecture, even when it shakes ideas of authorship and the architect's role; and that new social codes and freedoms may carry promises as well as threats.

There is only one inescapable reality — complex and multi layered — which is undergoing transformations that might change it beyond recognition. We do not have answers as to whether these changes will be for better or worse. All we do know is that whatever currents do form in style, they will emerge from increasing freedom and be shaped by our collective care.

UNREST. Does architecture appreciate a generative method of thinking? We consider the notion of generative thinking as a progression of architectural thought, yet the world of developer lead commerce looks at it financially. Thus, most architectural performance looks at the programming of architecture as something trivial and almost as a set of instructions. Do you fully believe that architecture can be designed through a set of simple

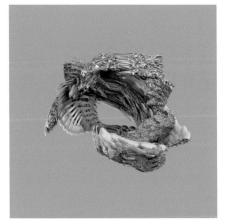

AESTHETICS OR A DEVALUED CONTRIBUTION. Are we so consumed by our own philosophical and conceptual retort as architects that we fail to consider aesthetics as meaningful thought? If the public appreciate architecture with the respect of liking the color or form — should we as architects not question these *"subjective qualities"*? Do we really think so highly of ourselves that the way that most people appreciate architecture is inherently wrong? Should we really dismiss aesthetics as only a subjective game?

instructions and become a generative money-maker? We oppose this retrograde notion of architecture.

DESIGNING WITH YOUR EYES SHUT.
Is it possible or borderline ridiculous? From time to time, we see design process regarded as a reasonably practical set of processes; as architects, we too often regurgitate practices and get lost in details. When the process is done we have forgotten the initial idea or overall conceptual ambition. The intuitive motion of the hand could help to express emotions replicating the seismograph — evoking natural feelings. Embrace the power of the accidental. Encouraging the desires of German Romanticism, reaffirming value to the emotional response within architecture. We must be more spontaneous in order to discover new forms of architecture.

Obj.1—3

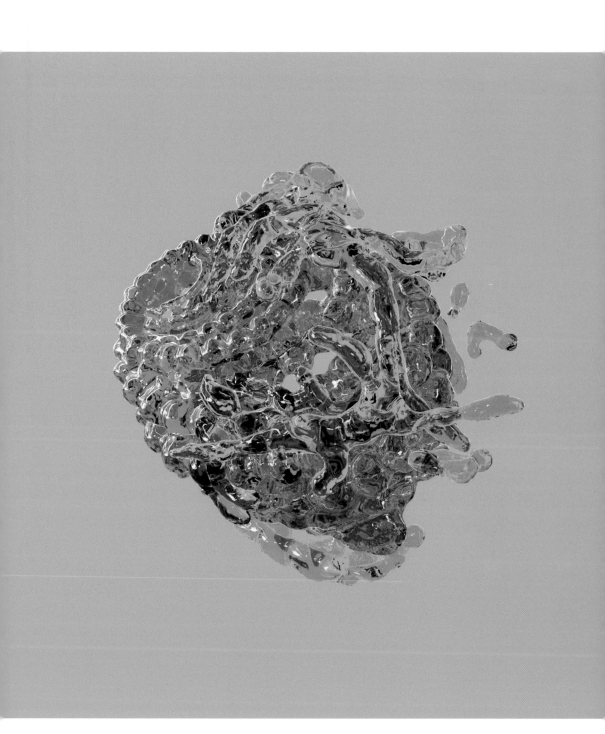

Obj. 4

SHOCKINGLY BANAL. Why are you frightened by *Schumacher's* utopia? *Parametricism 2.0* argues for an architecture which is, *Modern*, clear, and *useful* via its interconnectedness and parametric derivation — with form as a by-product of this design process. However, such efficiency ignores, subjugates and loses all historical formal aesthetic qualities of ornamentation, playfulness and balance that harken back to the Gothic period having served as drivers of creativity and innovation within the built environment. Embracing the *sensual, slippery and inferable qualities of architecture* (as Mark Foster Gage described them) welcomes a new era of spatial interconnectedness and orientation via form.

OPEN-SOURCE ARCHITECTURE. How can the Architectural Object help us orient in today's overstimulated environment? The Internet has given us endless information, excessive innovation and undervalued security in anonymity, leading to lives oversaturated with content, often at the expense of deeper learning and stronger emotional connections. Architecture must learn how to act as a filter, both physically and metaphysically, by drawing on the benefits of this Information Age of big data and digitized tools, whilst at the same time have the sentimental nature to protect us as human beings.

POST-TRAUMATIC ARCHITECTURE. Where was architecture when we needed it most? Our objects exist between the optimism of experimentation and the critically depressed state of the new built environment we find ourselves in. We should not forget that crisis is productive; it can redirect an avant-garde creativity towards new outlets, new objects as well as new enemies. Architecture has historically been a powerful social tool (e.g. *Berlin Wall*), and we must be vigilant in teaching our Architectural Objects to embrace diversity rather than divide each other.

Obj. 5—6

IF THE MACHINE COULD FEEL. Complexity is no longer a limitation but an opportunity for architects and designers, raising the question if human error is a problem we must solve throughout design? More fundamentally – who are the designers of the future: human or machine? It may be too much of a risk, having a human person, adding human error to the well-oiled design machines. The machines greatness for calculation, analysis and generative modeling through real-time data only loses its weight through the lack of programmed sensory understanding. Without the knowledge of knowing, what may be considered beautiful or not, no machine will have the capabilities to design these sensory experiential spaces. Yet, why should it understand our anthropocentric orientation of beauty? Should we not be progressive enough to consider that a machine's concept of beauty matters within architecture?

CAPTIVE BEASTS. Is architectural privilege killing our creativity? The notion of captivity we resist is not through physical means but as captive of legislative and financial instruments. Architecture is the unwanted son of the conglomerate, and must fight and push to exceed the realm of building, vers une architecture. Further, architecture is often contained and only the privileged few can truly experience it – acceptance to the lobby is unsatisfactory. If architecture can lose its sense of commodity then it may be able to truly be free (and free for those that experience it)!

Obj. 7—8

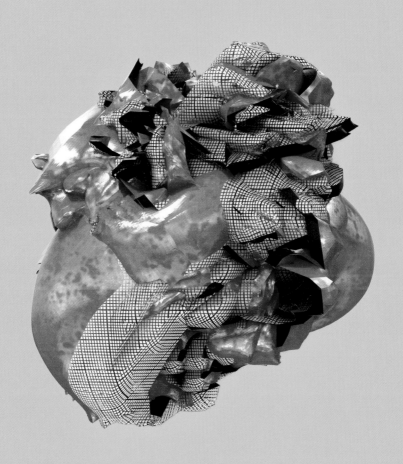

ARE WE IN CONTROL?
Descartes, *"cogito ergo sum,"*
relies on the idea that there is
no great overlord manipulating
our thoughts. Is architecture
the representation of critical
thought or the representation of
higher, otherworldly control?
Architecture, albeit possibly
contradictory, must direct
itself towards a socio-political
freedom as a catalyst of
change in our own dimension.

Obj. 9

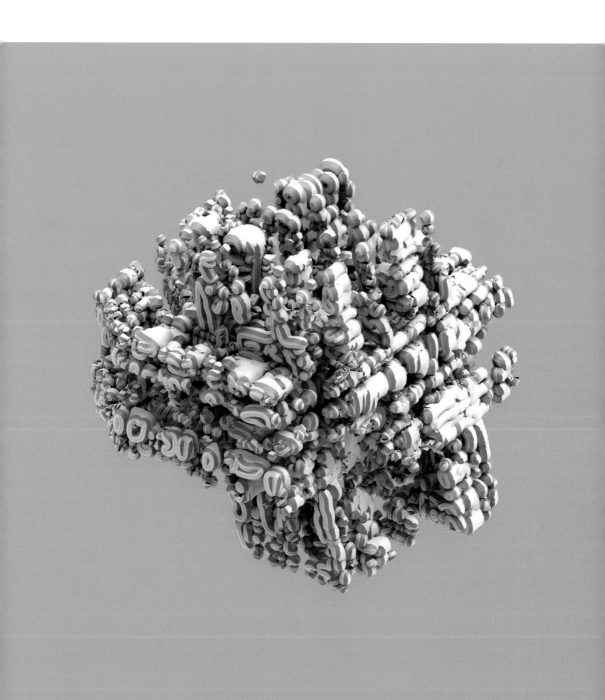

An Act of Rebellion

Obj. 10—12

THE INTELLIGENCE OF SYMMETRY. Can information gaps help us make more informed decisions? Our focus on new tools, data sets and processes to create an alternate language of/for: often non-vectoral geometries, which sit at the edge of aesthetics, spatial concepts and performance. However, innovation on numerous occasions, means incomplete and corrupted information. Nature deals with such situations by mechanisms of symmetry in emergent design; an attempt to bring order to chaos.

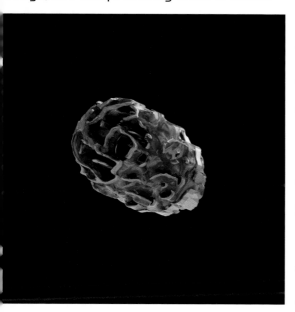

THE 5TH MOVEMENT. In a period of technological, social, cultural development, the so-called *Imagination Age,* why are we so consumed by nostalgia? Why must we make it great, again? Svetlana Boym aligns the thoughts and provocation of revolution with a societal nostalgia. As architects, we must reject the nature of pure nostalgia, where reiterations result in pastiche — we must yearn for a future developed by our past.

ARCHITECTURAL LANGUAGE. How do we refer to something without words? Everything has its own meaning, and therefore it is impossible to think without language. In a world without language, where would our Architectural Objects stand? *Derrida* rejected *Aristotle's, Socrates'* and *Plato's* idea of an objective truth, stating that our assumptions about objectivity are flawed. One must evaluate architectural writing regarding objects as well as the phenomenological experiences of architecture as an object.

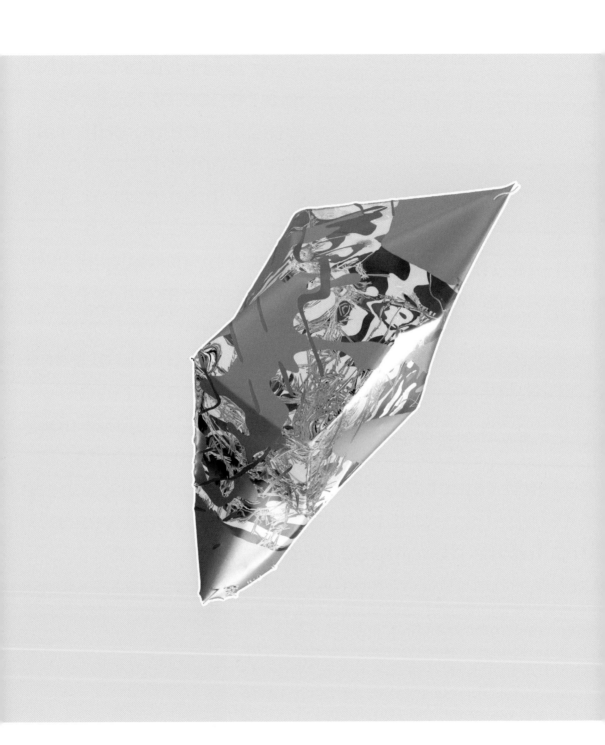

Obj.13

CRYPTIC IMAGERY. If someone hasn't posted it, does it exist? Consumed by imagery, our perception is formed by online stimulus to verify our existence. *Plato's Allegory of the Cave* is relevant when we consider how *"real"* something actually is; in this case we rely on realness through documentation online. Consider an architecture which cannot be documented virtually, completely invisible to machine vision, only perceivable through living beings' eyes. If the Internet, machine vision, AR and VR is the new reality – does architecture have time for phenomenological space or are these non-documentable spaces the revolution in our future existence?

EXISTENTIAL ARCHITECTURE. Have we lost something in our automation of design? Generative algorithms should be seen as tools for design and not designers in themselves. In 1950, *Alan Turing* asked us to *consider that computers can think,* but still today even our most advanced machine learning is specific and performance-driven. Thereby lacking a true understanding of our discipline's complexity and fundamentally requiring our architectural specificity.

WHO AM I. How do our Architectural Objects deal with the ephemeral nature of identity? Drawn — or scripted — too tight and they separate us from each other, yet, too loose and they fail to create meaningful connections. *Maurice Merleau-Ponty* has argued *that our understanding of the world is inextricable from the space around us,* and we agree, yet further insist that our architecture must flexibly explore, flirt and dance along this delicate divide for the survival of our discipline.

Obj. 14—15

INVISIBLE SURVEILLANCE. Is our obsession with oneself an expression of self-

LAYERS OF TRANSPARENCY. How can we understand a new formal language? Literal transparency is a well-established architectural and material concept, but more interestingly for us, is that newly encoded architecture has brought about the rise of an alternate *"phenomenal"* transparency. Mcuh in the smae way you can raed tihs sneetcne. A ptaetrn-bsaed or aglrotihimc-odreerd aprpaoch can gvie tarnpsraecny as udnretsandnig to a new froaml lnaugage of Acrhtiecutre.

narration or self-submission to a higher power? *Michel Foucault*, expressed our current state of existence as a *"confessing society"* – if we confess everyday, are we subsequently allowing ourselves to be controlled? Everyday architecture acts as a beacon, a hotspot for social confession. Can architecture be invisible or must it confess?

MATTER AND ENERGY. How can thermodynamics impact our design philosophy? As architects we strive to improve our thermodynamic performance in design, yet, take for granted that we exist in an open, non-isolated system in which form is nothing more than a struggle for entropy. In this sense, we must depar Cartesian and Eulerian planes to embrace something more Lagrangian — multi-dimensional.

ADAPT. Can architects truly adapt to the future? Our generation may be the first to see interplanetary exploration, and must adapt to new realms of possibilities. Architects must set the example for what is possible. To ensure that the pedagogy of architecture schools is complicit, acceptance that the world is developing will be the first step. We must relinquish sentimental ties with Modernism and look beyond its early 20th century context. Knowing how to develop architecture on Mars, will very soon become more important than knowing how to detail your parents' conservatory.

THE JUXTAPOSITION OF *THE SMOOTH* AND *THE STRIATED*. How can spaces thrive at the edge of this Deleuzian distinction? The wild smooth space is nomadic, dynamic and constantly being consumed by its *Stately* counterpart. It's precisely this juxtaposition and contradiction that enriches each in isolation as well as in combination. Let us not strive for efficient boredom but for a richer architectural and spatial experience.

Obj. 18—20

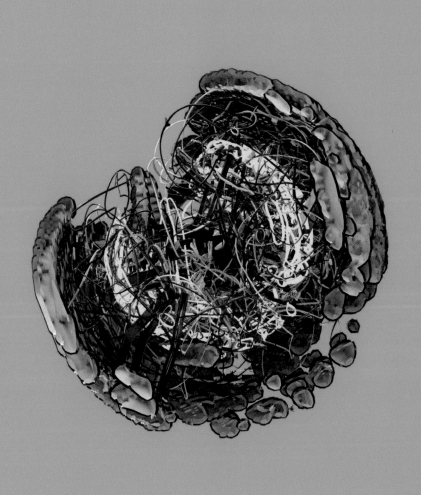

VAPORWARE. Is the Architectural Object destined to be deadstock? It lives in a realm of the *unknown*, a reality of confusion and mostly discontent. It embellishes the traits of 80s TV show memorabilia. Living in a realm of color, aesthetics and all-round Internet culture. It stands

DISCONTINUOUS EVOLUTION. Do mixed realities in architecture create a paradox for our physical designs? Until recently, a remote island in the pacific was visited by thousands of Google Earth explorers. The island's mysterious black surface attracted interest that ultimately led to its disappearance when an Australian research vessel confirmed its non-existence. It was identified as a glitch by Google Earth and removed from the world. Our architecture increasingly exists as both physical and digital objects, risking deletion as much as demolition. What do we consider to be *real* architecture?

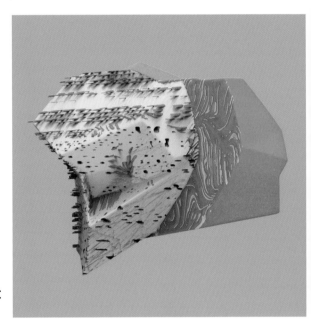

up for the weird, as an architectural subculture in a physical world, where form follows function and design follows cost. Unlike the Postmodernists, the object is here to stay. It lives comfortably in a world where it does not have to be defined solely by the physical. Its fluidity between the physical and the digital and everything in between gives the object an edge over its *"aesthetic"* predecessors.

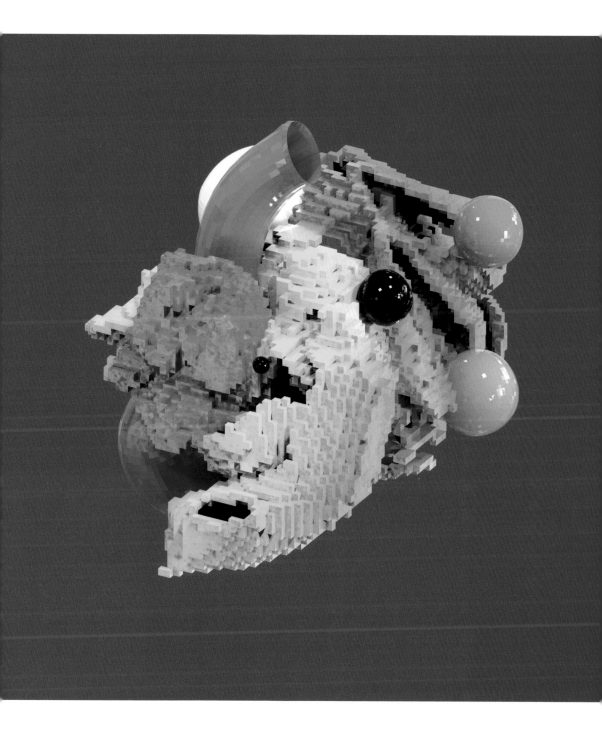

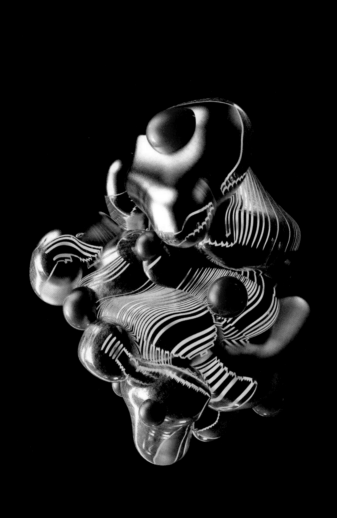

MEME. [1] How does meme culture affect architecture? Theoretical architectural stagnation is a common topic with little significant culture or theory is being developed through books or papers. Our answer to this is *"obviously."* The profession is growing rapidly under the radar of most. Daily, new hashtags, new Instagram accounts and new memes are causing invigorating discussion and progress in the field. Do not abide by the rules. Do not believe that only the books and papers produced, by those with accreditation, are important. Architecture is more than ever developing an openly underground culture — digitally.

ARCHITECTURE AS OBJECTS. What is our obsession with the Architectural Object? We find merit in a new approach towards architectural identity not as a facilitator of space but as space in itself — the same idea we can apply to ourselves as objects within an architecture. In this context, it is fitting to create architecture in advancing ways including (but not limited to); physical simulation and metaphysical systems.

STRUCTURAL SINGULARITY. How can structure and imbalance coexist? We believe singularities in architecture are no longer about tectonics and instead focus on a distribution of differentials. Therefore, in our quest for morphogenesis as well as new qualities, we must look to structure not as a means of establishing rational evenness, but rather a tool for pushing design away from equilibrium and into something imbalanced, sensitive and creative.

1

Memes are low-quality images with text caption overlays (often in an Impact typeface) which are widely distributed through online platforms (e.g. 9GAG, 4chan, Reddit, Instagram, Facebook). More importantly — memes are a form of mass culture developed entirely on the Internet, making them one of the first 'post-digital' inventions. (Cramer, Florian)

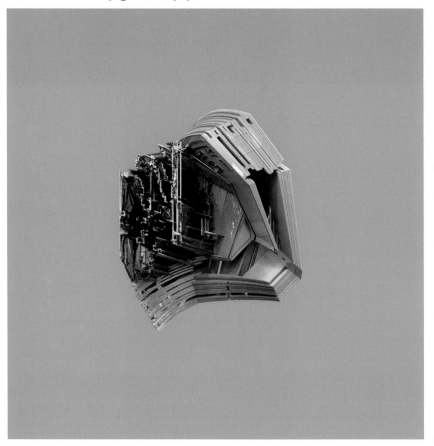

NEURAL NARRATIVES. How did we get here? Our use of neural networks and generative algorithms increasingly deliver results without an underlying explanation. Relying on such processes often can propel our designs forward. Nevertheless, they will fundamentally change the way we explain our final results. Perhaps, as our tools

WITH OPEN ARMS. Should we be skeptical of the open-source community? Open-source communities have been instrumental in creating rapid change across tech industries, but architecture — ever frightened of the unknown and cautious to give up ownership have been reluctant to indulge. We believe architects must fully grasp the nature of open-source communities in order to steer those networks in a direction towards a prosperous exciting new epoch of architectural thought via collaboration. Is the steering of ships the new role of the architect?

become artificially intelligent we will rely on them to explain the design to us — undermining our both understanding of the processes and threatening our control of their outcomes.

Obj. 26—27

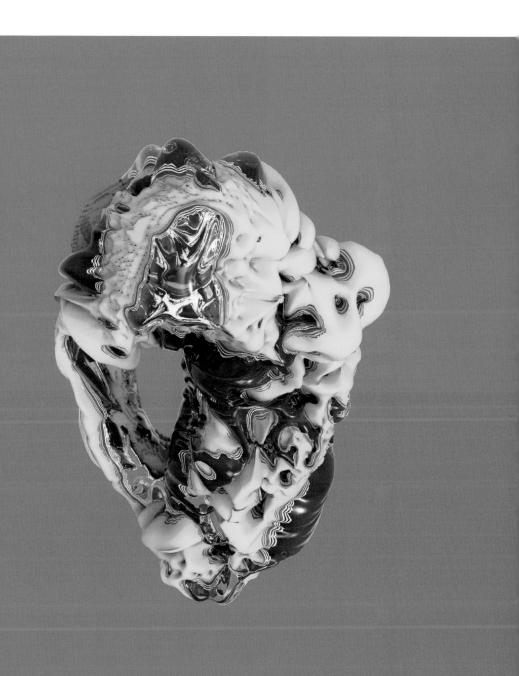

COMMUNICATION IN ARCHITECTURE.

How do we communicate essential information architecturally without ugly signage? Advertisements and signs have invaded our cities, having a major influence on our choices, preferences and navigation — acting as constant visual noise. The Las Vegas Strip is an example of a commercial architecture which has to coerce customers to its premises by looking attractive, more colorful and tackier. We as architects despise such visual crimes and believe we have to learn to deliver information by expression of form and texture rather than banners and sloppy slogans which are brandishing our cities with useless junk. Instead of bolting

COMMAND.

How does architecture direct other doctrines? *David Byrne* of *Talking Heads* express-es *that music is designed for architecture and not the opposite*. Thus, if our creative doctrine can command itself towards a more progressive environment, architecture itself could subsequently invent new movements within music. Consider the notion of working not for acoustic pleasure but for an environment where specific sounds can be embellished and thus the music itself must become one with the architecture — unable to be fully explored without the space. Architecture, must command all sensory aspects of space.

N-DIMENSIONS.

Is there a limit to experiencing architecture? Bernard Tschumi said, *"There is no way to perform architecture in a book. Words and drawings can only produce paper space, not the experience of real space."* Tschumi, arrives at the idea wherein two dimensions are not enough to experience architectural space, fully. Considering this, of course, the 3rd dimension starts to engage in a realm of space beyond the 2nd, but more importantly plays on the idea of ephemeral space, which to most is indescribable, yet vivid. We believe that there are multiple dimensions which can be explored through innovative technologies, yet, their importance alongside their positioning within phenomenological space remains unclear.

on these neon signs and Coca-Cola branding, Architectural Objects must embrace these motifs and act as icons for our cities, truly embodying pop culture.

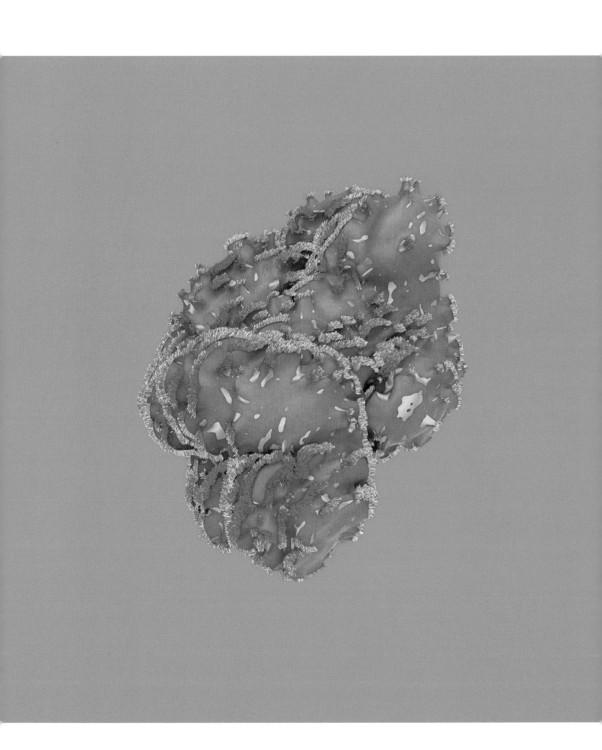

THE GEO-METRI-CIAN.

"Let no one enter who is not a Geome-

THE VISUAL VOCABU-LARY OF OBJECT-ORIENTED ARCHITEC-TURE. Does machine learning combined with agent-based systems enable a more intelligent design paradigm? Let us expose flaws in *'Parametricism 2.0'* by eluding the performative, in search of the image, as the first truly architectural concept. Let us place the machine in a gothic cathedral and begin our disruption of this current era of architecture.

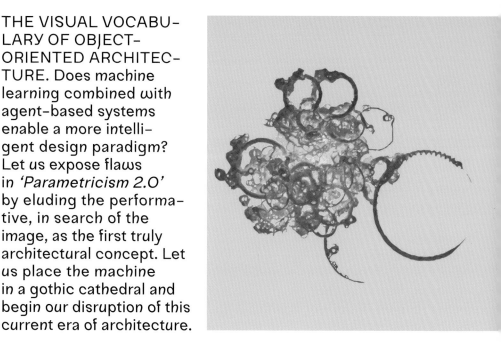

trician" was inscribed above the entrance to Plato's academy. To what level are we described by our knowledge of the

UGLY. Is *ugly* the new beautiful? Over the last 100 years, we have embraced function over decoration, embracing the nature of functional formal beauty. No longer should we be obsessed with functional form and the production of it. The era of this beauty has passed, and now we may embrace the ugly. Reject the notion of perfection. It is a lie and it is boring. The object finds itself, through the motions of a disgruntled architectural period. Embrace the language that has been neglected. Embrace your ugliness. The object has, so why can't you?

Object? Peter Sloterdijk expressed, "Philosophy begins by splitting society into those who remember and those who do not." Should the Architectural Object and our knowledge of its geometry underpin and divide us as those who know and those who don't? This idea questions whether we can ever understand more than the surface nature of the object. An object may be readable to those *who do not know* as well as those who do. The object must be a unifier not a divider of people, of culture and of space.

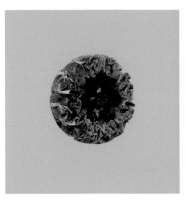

SCENARIO X. The use of Virtual Reality within architecture raises questions, whether it is actually architecture or not. Where does the delineation of architecture begin or end? Architecture is not attached to physicality, it is about creating experiences through systems and constructs. Through spaces, we define people's actions, habits, identities and behaviors. Virtual Reality is about adding another dimension of reality where we, as architects, have greater control of each scenario and its experience via simulation. Within this reality, architects are not confined by any rules of our current reality. This post-physical reality is about creating human experience, dynamically and by taking people to other realities with new levels of consciousness beyond the confines of the physical. Defining features of these worlds, allow the architect full control of their reality's environment, gravity and materiality become obsolete rules and relationships.

OUR REALITY: YOUR REALITY. Consider each person living within their own *"bubble"* – in the sense that they have their own perceptions of the world and how they understand or perceive objects. We understand these individual experiential opinions as a reality. Therefore, do we all live within our own reality, and if so can this be altered or extended? Architecture is at a crucial moment where it is transitioning from the realm of the physical to that of the digital, both augmented and entirely virtual. This is the beginning of an experience-based architecture. Where space moves towards more immersive theoretical understanding of reality and where shared vs. individual experiences will become critical.

ARTEFACTS. Do architectural monuments depict our past? *Aldo Rossi* insists that the city remembers its past through its monuments. Expanding on this notion, one questions the nature in which Architectural Objects can influence or create a story both past, present and in the future of the city. These objects can and will act as narrative triggers depicting a past that may not exist or a future that will not arrive. The autonomy of these monumental storytellers and the manipulation of the stories they tell — becomes an important consideration at their birth.

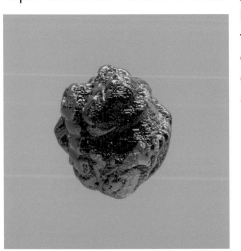

Obj. 34—36

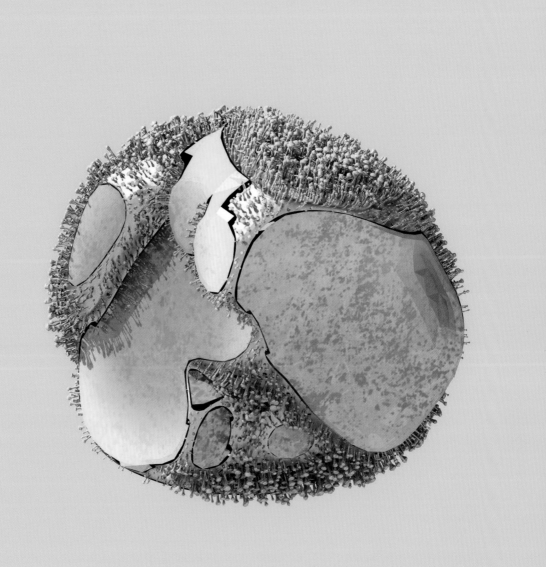

AMORPHIC ARCHITECTURE. How can the pairing of computational design and material systems enable tectonic possibilities? The integration of material behavior into algorithmic thought both enables and combats the idea that materials are seen as *'shapeless,'* equiring additional construction systems like form to work. Using these digital tools combined with cyber–physical production systems, we may avoid the traditional singular readings of materials within formal, spatial, and structural articulation.

DUALITY IS DYING. How do we make sense of too many conflicting desires? We live in an unprecedented era of competing ideas, mixed realities, technological competition and political populism. Such dichotomies can be exhausting for designers and risk diluting our intentions at ever–greater rates with increased efficiency. *Mark Titman* claimed *that while we live in a time of dualities, we also exist on the brink of a new era;* and at this crucial moment it is important for us as architects to reflect and synthesize such splits so as to work progressively, rather than derivatively.

RECONSTRUCTIVISM. Is it time to put back together everything we fractured during the '80s? The glorification of structuralism, which has influenced architecture throughout the preceding four decades, has distracted us and led our discipline on a wild goose chase, bringing us closer to engineers than architects. Without a doubt, these explorations have led to both incredible advances and impressive work, but the game is over and it's time to get serious about space again.

TIMELESS ARCHITECTURE. Is there such a thing? If so, what does it mean? A structure, which stands for centuries may find itself at odds with a design concept that does not resonate with new generations. The allure of timeless architecture inspires us to push boundaries beyond the physical presence of an object. However, this must be balanced against an embrace of the ephemeral nature of our discipline. We argue an embrace of architecture's mutability — to remain truthful to time itself by letting our structures age, erode and stain. While at the same time reflecting their concepts for generations to come despite their changing conceptual context.

Obj. 39—40

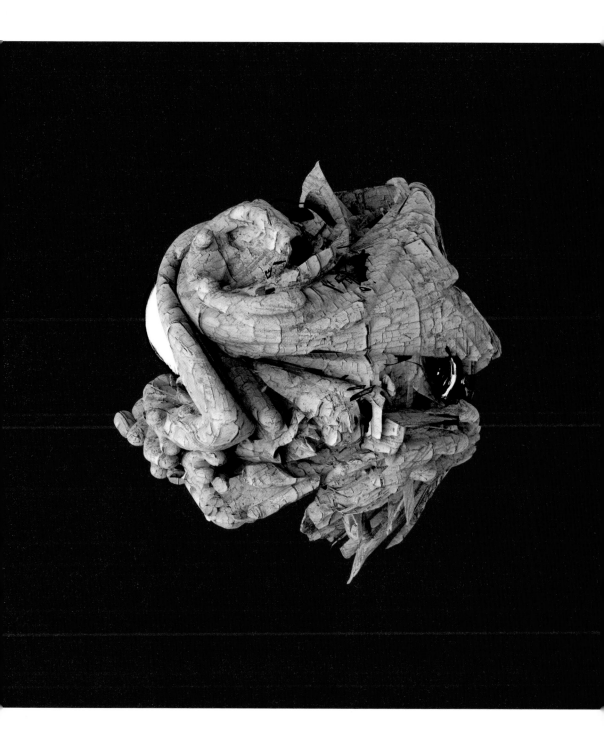

REASONABLE DIMENSIONS. If we remain focused within the realm of 2.5D and 3D, will we lose our sense of reason and materialism? *Søren Kierkegaard* opposed reason, stating it *does not give us what we want: meaningful lives.* Further, *Kierkegaard* expressed that a leap of passion should replace reason. Architecture can regain its passion, overcoming the realm of reason to seek out ideas born of essentialism. We must make a passionate leap toward an architecture where its essence, is known prior to its existence.

CHAOS OR GEOMETRIC ORDER. Should we incorporate ideal relationships like symmetry, parallelism and the golden ratio within our designs or should we stick to the opposite, complex and convoluted notions? It is natural for these

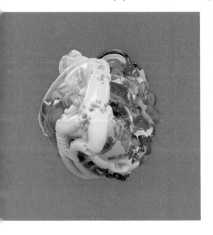

ONTOGENESIS OBJECT. Are we in a state of post fertilization, with no clear path of growth? Each Architectural Object we design becomes a catalyst for socio-political change or in fact just change itself, if one considers the Butterfly Effect then, *"everything you do matters."* Are our architectural explorations deconstructing our contractor-based future — where architecture begins to matter, again? Yes. Whatever can happen, will happen.

two opposite definitions to not coexist together. We thrive for the unexpected and a chaotic architecture, which not only changes our perception of space where contrast can never leave anyone indifferent.

Obj. 41—43

Obj. 44—45

WHAT DO YOU WANT, BRICK? *Louis Kahn* states, *"a brick likes an arch."* Yet we question the singular function of materiality and their personality. Architecture must consciously profess material shifts towards an ever-expanding world, wherein the Cartesian world can meet that of the Lagrangian. Where the brick, no longer needs to like an arch but can manifest itself as a blob instead. We must take on this simple notion of flux within and as *Michel Foucault* argues *we must rethink our history as a way to see our future and the objects within it.*

ACTIVE MATERIALS. How can digital models advance physical material properties? Computation allows us to move beyond Louis Kahn's notion of bricks as arches. Parametric models offer the potential to delve deeper, into the complex characteristics of

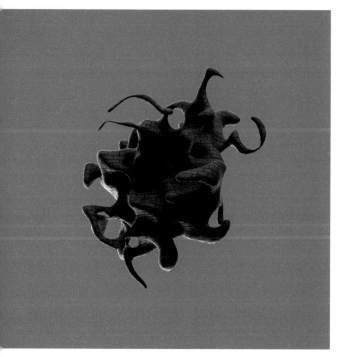

material rules and thereby redefine them from a passive receptor of predefined form into an active participant in design. This fundamentally challenges established preconceived rules of nature.

THE EXCHANGE. Have we exchanged the ephemeral qualities of architecture for that of an intellectualized babble? The hope of our peers tugging us off, spurs on our exacerbated language and thinking. In order to ground ourselves once more, a firm understanding of people and our needs must truly be explored. It is imperative that we do not lose focus, and lose touch with those we are truly designing for.

THE CLOUD OR THE CLOCK. Can we really *understand* space? As architects assisted by advanced technology, we blindly believe that we exert a strong level of control over our design process. Even convincing ourselves we have programmed the idea of randomness; yet physicists continue to debate the very nature of our surroundings. Let us take inspiration from the blurred boundaries of *Newtonian* and *Quantum* theories and trust in our intuition, our exuberance and our emotions to embrace the messiness of the Cloud.

ALTERNATE. How does popular culture influence our visions of the future? Visions of the future are drastically distorted by media. *Le Corbusier's Weißenhofsiedlung 14 & 15* embodies a future from the late 1920s but appears almost current, and even exciting to this day. Perhaps our longing for nostalgia is defining our visions of the future. Our nostalgic nature is not a burden but a gift to explore the nature of pop culture through design, wherein we have a mixed future of tech that is not simply focused on the performance, yet discusses aesthetics and form.

Obj. 46—48

A NEW CONVERSATION.

THE BOUNDARY OF AN ARCHITECTURAL OBJECT.

Some consider it to be a façade or the thermal envelope, but is there a boundary at all? We live in an open thermodynamic system, where matter and energy freely exchange with their surroundings. Therefore, we can consider architecture being in constant flux; moving, intersecting and dissecting itself as a constant reorganization of its own matter. With all this stated, can we even consider architecture through x, y, z and time or must we completely forget our traditional limits of reality?

What is the role of the Architect? Perhaps the single most amazing thing about parametricism is that it created an identity crisis within our profession and thereby sparked conversations about space again, albeit hidden in the term *"geometry."* As our ownership models and design tools are fluidly changing, we must remember that our core competencies lie in the sensual inferable qualities of space and the object, irrespective of their narrative.

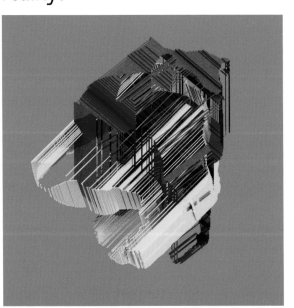

Obj. 49—50

EVOLUTION OF AESTHETICS. Is historical nostalgia reducing our impression of beauty to one of Cartesian order? In *1753, Marc-Antoine Laugier* suggested that architectural beauty could be achieved through *absolute perfection in proportion and order* – a belief based on classical canons such as those of *Palladio* and *Vitruvius*. However, such an approach reduces aesthetics to a certain formal association of discrete parts, whereas we argue that aesthetics is compelled to reflect a more authentic approach, which will enhance the continuity of our existence –

ARCHITECTURE ISOLATION. Why do people feel isolated and disconnected when we have greater technological connectivity than ever before? Technology has somehow both brought us together and split us apart, as evident not only in our discipline but in the ever-fracturing populist world around us. Architectural Objects with their inherent mix of human values and technological makeup have a responsibility to use complexity of form in order to expose us to new vantage points, connecting us further as people. Beyond this, we believe that fragmenting and the disruption this divide has enabled, is precisely integrated within a new formal language which objects inherently embody.

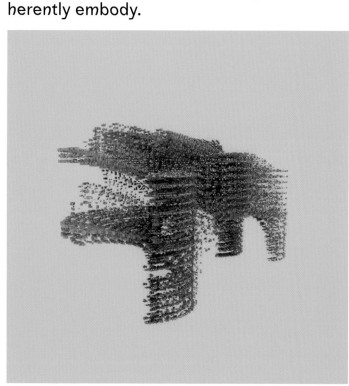

the embedded intelligence of our design approach and the exploration of a new-found optimism.

CLINT EASTWOOD ARCHITECTURE.
How does Pop Cult$\underline{ure}_2$ influence Architecture? It forces anons and Internet personalities to share their opinion, comment, like or dislike it. The Internet unveils the restrictions, IRL, which gives birth to discussions, arguments as well as collaborations. When the fabrication process is completely automated by robots and machines, perhaps it will be possible that the buildings are designed and built remotely by crowds from all corners of the world. We think when a building is designed by very different individuals anonymously, without previous knowledge what architecture should be — that is when architecture will fully embrace Pop Culture. Where the good, the bad and ugly of reality, and even worse the digital, meet.

Obj. 53

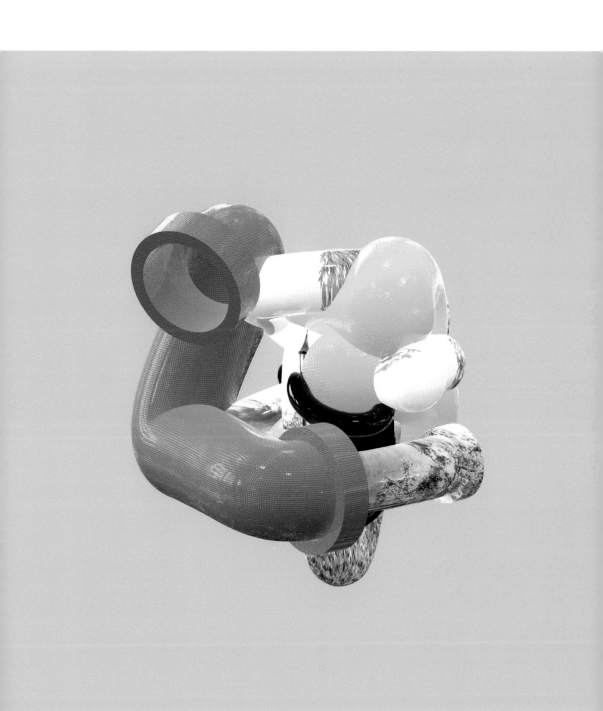

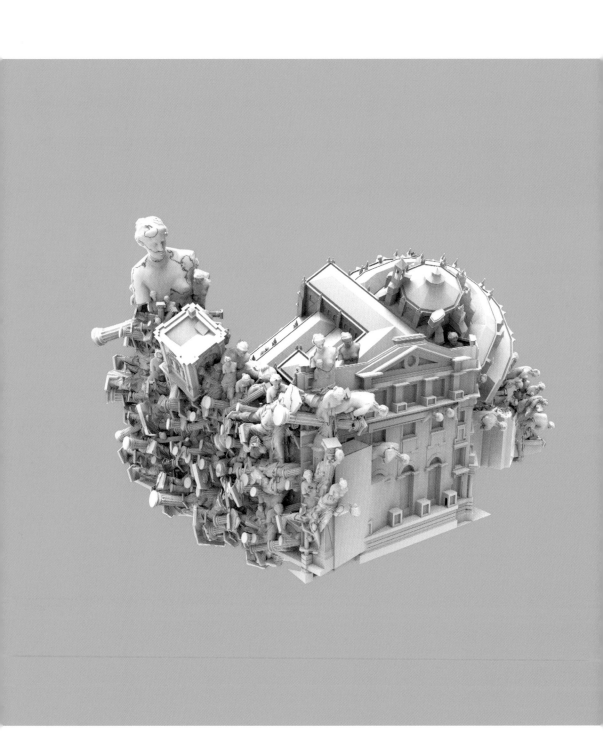

NEONEOCLASSICISM. What is the role of order and proportion in architecture today? Our discipline is founded upon golden rules of relationship, hierarchy and beauty. Though few students — and even fewer architects — are able to cantillate them. In our digital age, it is easy to dismiss such adages as too simple or lacking a modern conceptual basis. And yet these structures have proven themselves timeless and unassailable. We can reinvent these enduring structures through an ephemeral object-oriented approach wherein classical form evolves to engender new spaces.

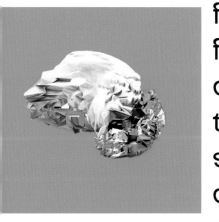

A THOUGHT ON ALGORITHMIC THOUGHT. What if algorithmic computation is not simply a mathematical tool, but rather a mode of thought in its own right? We find inspiration in Luciana Parisi's new vocabulary of design including forms which lie beyond human cognition or control. The power of generative abstraction can be rivaled only by the complexities of the real world.

MUTERATION. Where do our ideas reside? As the boundary between what is alive and what is machine becomes increasingly blurred, we must hold on to our creative curiosity whilst fostering new relationships between all participants in the design process. The balance we strike between machine learning, experimentation and failure will come to define how our Architectural Objects interact with each other, their contexts and ourselves.

OVER 18. Is architectural censorship truly a problem? With the prominence of architecture as a tool for oppression and distinction in totalitarian states we question the almost safe – conservative – role of architecture within 'free' western societies. At a global level, architecture has lost the fight with traditional finance, and m² ultimately becomes the dictation of 2D expression. Architecture has always been censored by financial greed [3] or flamboyant with political immorality. Cities today focus more on economy than architecture.

HUMAN EROSION. What is sacred in the age of the Anthropocene? Biodigital design may be one of the only tools we have left to create truly sustainable structures. Pairing natural and artificial systems at different resolutions and scales may enable our architectural and urban principles to flourish in a way which is not damaging to the planet. To accomplish this goal we must grapple with the integration of thermodynamics, robotics, and natural sciences into an emergent and adaptive design process.

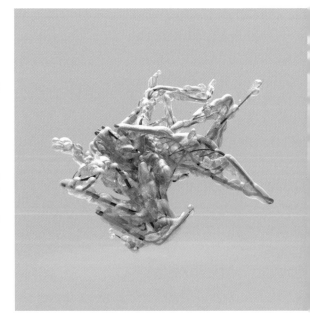

Obj. 56—58

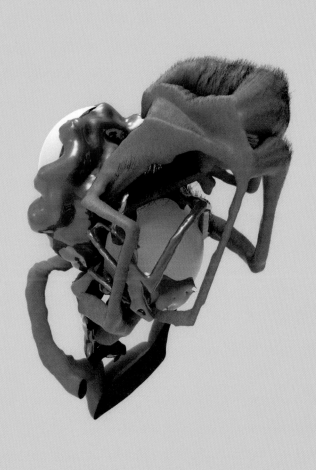

─────3

"These spaces are highly tuned machines
for making money in." (Holm, Lorens,
"Architecture is (not) interested in wellbeing")

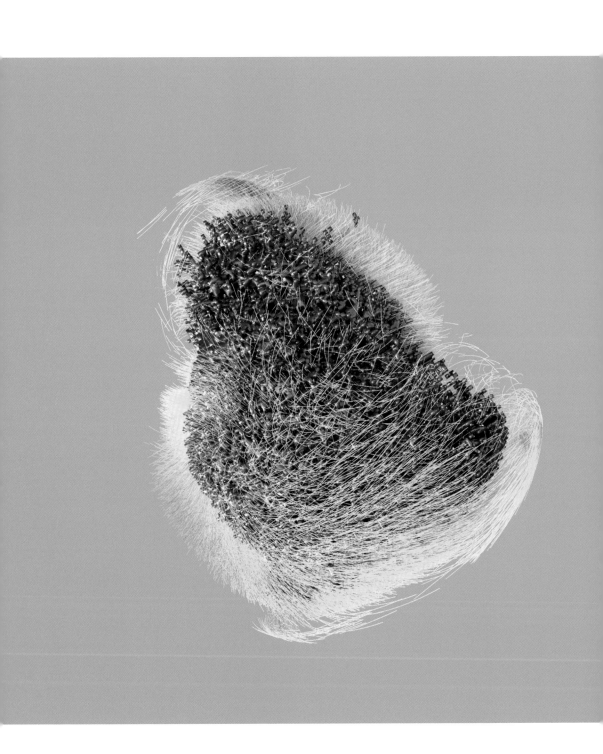

Obj. 59—61

ISOLATED NOW. Is the focus on a guiding architectural movement beneficial or detrimental? Since the 60s no strong definitive architectural statement has helped us navigate. Instead of perpetuating along an outstanding idea within a movement, long forgotten, we should develop what architecture is now. This should be evident through our expanding process and the objects we create. We are defining our reality through *isolated now's*.

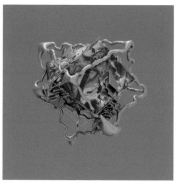

STEP BACK. Ask yourself: what is your purpose, can you bring meaning into life? Chaos within social and political life is frequently overwhelming at best. It puts architecture last on any list — it isn't relevant at all. Architects decide that it isn't the time for great spatial discoveries or speculative theoretical concepts. A different scenario: *Lebbeus Woods' seminal Sarajevo work* embodies the horror of *War and Architecture*, these explorations encouraged important speculative discussions. His proposals are somehow beautiful and ugly at the same time. Beautiful as the perfection of objects, and ugly as a representation of fear and horror of events in Sarajevo. We need to act upon what is happening in our world. Now is precisely the time for architectural discovery!

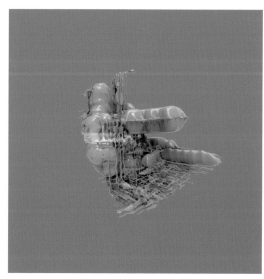

ARCHITECTURAL HIERARCHY. Do we have the legs to stand on? Architecture, the judgmental snob, acting like it understands the world and acting as if it has only one answer. In academia, they fight over who is correct, yet who has given them this authority. Architecture must be humble, accepting as well as adventurous. Not to be swayed in a certain direction because of its peers obnoxious opinions. Architecture serves the people and we must utilize our ideas to propel a future of acceptance and progression. If not, architecture will dissolve into a large argument of pseudo-intellect and lose all focus of its true meaning.

TRANSDIMENSIONAL REALISM. What do you believe is real? *Plato* argued that we *could understand the realm of being as something that is subjective.* The parallels

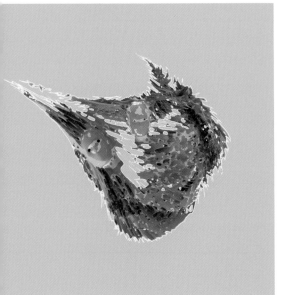

CONTROL. Are we defined through our facial qualities, in form and color or is this, again, an attempt to divide? *Zach Blas' Facial Weaponization Suite: Mask* touches on the notion of *weaponization* of devices to condemn control; control of our sexualities and our race. We challenge the nature in which the Architectural Object can embody these changes; rejecting cctv surveillance; rejecting the confines of mass media outlets and big business influence. Seeking an open spatial condition. This new condition, not in form but in theory, it will be a means of escape from the terms and conditions which situate us in a state of capitalist control.

of technology to this concept of what is real allows for questioning through the realm of Augmented Reality and Virtual Reality as new realities. For architects and occupants alike, this new *real* which is constantly hidden, and opens another dimension of design and activation. Architecture must appreciate, exploit and interpret this new dimension of life.

Obj. 62—63

SEMIOTIC AGENTS. How should we use system simulations? Agent-based parametric models give us the deterministic abilities to forecast precise scenarios from gallery vernissages to stadium evacuations, but precision and reality are far from the same truth. Undoubtedly, scripting enables entirely new realities both performative and formal — a captivating opportunity for us. But we should also remember, that our underlying semiological systems are inherently susceptible to random creativities both unwanted as well as those desired. Embracing this can allow for new cultural activities and limit unforeseen dangers.

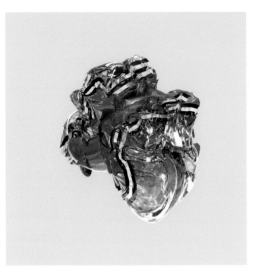

RETURN OF THE FOLD. How can Architectural Objects reinterpret the *Deleuzian* notion of *fusional multiplicity*? Whilst many Architectural Objects seem to reject inter-weaving and interconnectedness of form — this is not a full reflection. The conceptual rejection is one of heterogeneous continuity, rather than a question of composition or posture.

GIVING LIFE. Do new fabrication technologies transfer consciousness into architecture? As ever-intelligent design principles are applied to architecture, we increasingly find that the objects we create have digital lives of their own. We now expect the same thinking to follow advances in fabrication, when coupled with objects as sentient structures. Further, this prompts us to consider what are the ramifications of this sentient structure living among us.

In fact, an object's freedom from such continuity gives it a richer opportunity to incorporate complexity through the inclusion of disparate characteristics from constituent parts. An idea, we believe, to be an apt reinterpretation of *Deleuze's* notion of *externality internalization*, yet, from a far more spatial perspective.

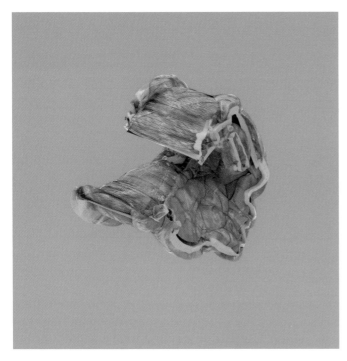

OCCUPANCY. How can architects contribute to fixing the housing crisis? Only 18% of people live in homes over 20 m². The rest have inappropriate and often hazardous living conditions. We must dedicate time to developing an open source affordable architecture — smart self-buildable homes — which may be self-sufficient, self-powered as well as self-repairing. We must finally decide the priorities within architectural research. By combining technology, community involvement and research we can finally start giving everyone the same opportunity for a good life with a safe home.

LOCALISM. Have we all but forgot about the idea of *localism* within architecture? Today, you view renders on mass-produced devices, made up of parts from diverse nations and ultimately, we are subjugated by commerce. This propaganda has infested our architectural interventions worldwide where glass towers are erected effortlessly lacking any relationship to culture or cultural appreciation through architecture. Localism is not necessarily contextual, and architecture must embody the nature of specific cultures through its objects regardless of location.

Obj. 67—68

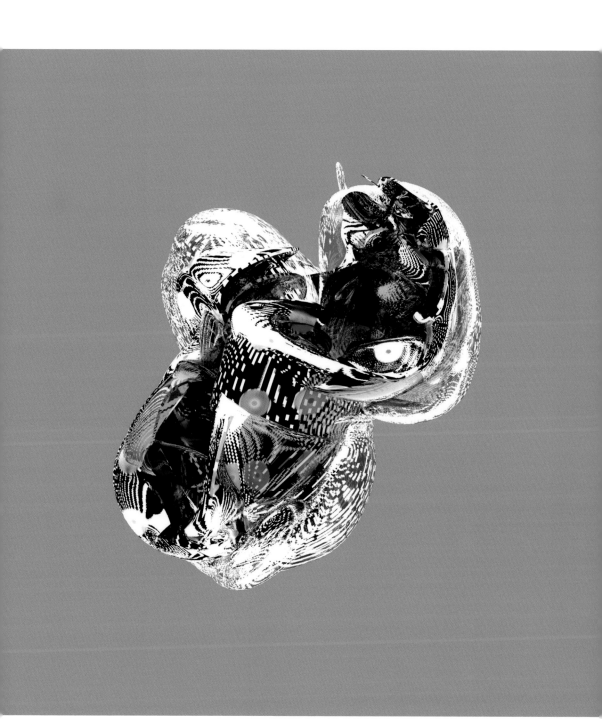

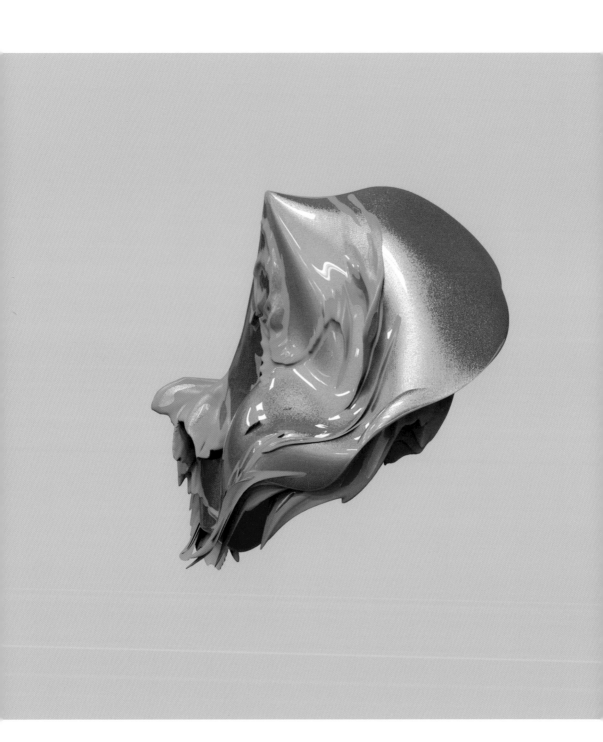

ENIGMATIC OBJECTS. Are you practicing or promoting? *Ian Bogost* expresses concern for those who are *expanding their philosophy due to capitalistic concerns*. He iterates that object construction is as important as writing itself. We believe in a similar notion, where, the Architectural Object

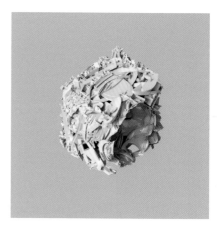

finds itself both as a manifestation of our theory and vice versa, the theory

EXPERIMENTAL TOOLS IN ARCHITECTURE. Is coding in architecture having a detrimental effect on the personality of projects? Coding in architecture has opened a lot of doors where architects define sets of rules whilst the code develops an outcome. But should architects rely on code so much? We find ourselves at a pivotal point wondering if we call ourselves architects when the design process may happen out of reach? We, as architects, believe it is important to be in control of the tools you are utilizing. With the development of technologies, such as Augmented Reality and Virtual Reality, architecture is regaining an artistic component of the profession. Giving architects more tactile control over the design process. With a knowledge of how these technologies are advancing will allow us full control of their direction.

ARCHITECTURAL UTOPIA. Early modernists believed that architecture was the key to our socio-political enlightenment, solving our key, world problems. However, currently the day-to-day life of an architect seems less glamorous and ultimately less important. Have we lost the utopianistic spirit of the early Modernists? Those that saw glorious futuristic towers fit for all and the automobile taking the world by storm. We must engender the spirit of these utopian Modernists, again, pushing architecture through material, social and philosophical means, where we are thriving for a future beyond this era of catalogue architecture.

is a manifestation of the object itself. For us the theory and the construct are one in the same.

BIFURCATION POINTS IN ARCHI-TECTURE. To what extent do endless options limit our design abilities? Our algorithmic approach towards archi-tecture has opened up unprecedented flexibility: options beget more options, and iterative models produce endless results. In attempting to navigate an infinite terrain, we find the scientific concept of *bifurca-tion points* intriguing: imagine confining our scripts such that at each branching point, the options are well defined but the choice is arbitrary. In such a way we may open new systems of design that while identical at the outset can end up on quite dif-ferent branches — experiencing the same driving forces, yet, creat-ing clarity in their distinction.

X, Y OR Z. How can architecture communicate its non-Carte-sian derivation? Our discipline faces the interesting challenge of having tools and technolo-gies which allow us to design in *Lagrangian* and *Eulerian* spa-tial systems, and yet, in showing these designs on 2D media we find it nearly impossible to use anything but a Cartesian system. This oversimplifies the intelligence of the design process thereby limiting the design itself. We suggest that multiple si-multaneous perspectives and the use of mixed reality devices are already key to architecture explanation.

DIGITAL VANDALISM. What is Digi-tal Vandalism and to what extent can digital intrusions affect architects today? Today the youth plot aug-mented constructs within cities, invisi-ble to most, if not all. Architects and activists have the ability to com-municate knowledge and experi-ence through these uncharted digital cities and articulate the digital di-mension of a built fabric. These cities lay desolate, waiting for *'construction via compiling.'* We believe archi-tects should take advantage of our dig-ital age and allow their unbuilt works to occupy cities digitally pre-senting an alternative digital future.

Obj. 72—74

An Act of Rebellion

Obj. 75—77

ARCHITECTURE OF DESIRE. How do gender and sexuality shape space? *Bernard Tschumi* believed that *"Architecture cannot satisfy your wildest fantasies, but it may exceed the limits set by them."* In this sense, the Architectural Objects we design today can help build or erode sexual identity. Let us use this influence to tear down stereotypes, foster experimentation. Rather than closing ourselves off to each other by hiding our perversions — express ourselves outwardly.

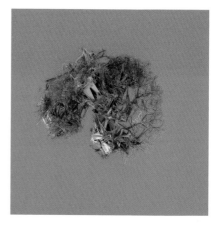

LONG LIVE THE GLITCH.
How do distortions and mistakes fit into the new visual language of architecture?

Glitches are like architectural instincts — partially understood, phenomenally transparent — stitched versions of a truth we cannot fully process. They press us as designers to step outside our comfort zone of understanding and explore new creative moments. Pushed from equilibrium, we believe these distortions offer cutting-edge ways to express and disseminate architectural ideas via physical form. Something that is often lacking in rigid Cartesian approaches and which is an alternative to utopic metaphysical realities.

POLIBLOBS. What is architecture's role in politics? The RFP (Request for Proposal) for Trump's border wall is officially out and it raises questions about architecture's political stance. Our responsibility as architects is to stand up for what is right. Our spaces drive and influence how we view the world around us; our objects must speak freely; they embrace diversity and oppose tyranny even when our leaders and our clients do not. Build tunnels beneath that <u>wall!</u> ₄

———— 4
"Freedom is the innermost dynamic of existence, and the very process of existence in an unfree world is the continuous negation of that which threatens to deny freedom." (Marcuse, Herbert)

ARCHITECTURE POSTURE.
What can *we* as architects learn from
Flemish Renaissance painters?
What if we personify our Architectural
Objects: allowing them to learn,
to hug, to fight? How do such moves
affect the spatial environment?
We find inspiration in the posture of
traditional artistic still life compo-
sitions; these classical rules reapplied
to a post-Cartesian, technology-
oriented design setting enables opportunities for object-oriented
architecture that bleeds beyond basic aesthetic principles, into emotional and spatial realms.

Obj. 18

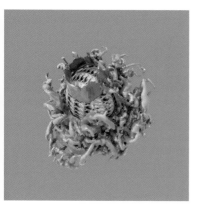

DIMINISHING INTELLI-GENCE. Will our future selves ever bother to learn new languages, try to drive or even think creatively thanks to the increasing artificial intelligence of new tools? As designers, the introduction of AI via generative design tools offers profound potential. Potential to uncover undiscovered forms and increase efficiency throughout our discipline. However, we must remain constantly vigilant, as new technologies often come with the allure of simplicity and the distraction of veiled complexity. Careful consideration of how we use these tools to further architecture's important theoretical concepts and core facets is necessary and increasingly overlooked both within our discipline as well as the world around us.

DO WHAT YOU CAN'T. Aren't we all academics now? Instagram. Facebook. Snapchat. YouTube. This is now the main form of contemporary and academic life. Geotagged Locations. Instagram Stories. Snapchat snaps. Facebook Live. Instagram LIVE. Everything LIVE. Your own urban movement logged online — by yourself or those who have filmed you. We believe these tools set fire to the academic paper and blaze trails for a future where there is no need to sit and mull over your intricate use of language, hoping to please editors or sponsors. We are our own editors. Share your own vision! The world has never been so open, so free.

9 BILLION. By 2050, our population will have increased to this. How can architects and thinkers combat the issues that come with exponential population growth? Climatically, we can address the concerns of renewables and zero carbon constructions, but is this really a seriously constructive approach? This suffers from symptoms of localization. Incorporation of thermodynamic principles can address the issues more conceptually in an attempt to reconfigure the world we live in as a whole — an open system whereby energy movements and relationships are inherently complex and interconnected. Our goal is to design spaces, which not only give people the power to survive in this world, but to thrive globally!

RANDOMNESS AND ERROR. Why are we so intrigued by glitches and distortions? While algorithms are feverishly regarded as precise and regulated, this is often far from the truth. The entropic tendency of data to increase in size, thus becoming random drives infinite amounts of information to interfere with and to reprogram algorithmic procedures. The resulting effects often hint both to an honest representation and an undiscovered creative one, which would be impossible for us as humans to predefine.

VIRTUOUS FREE-DOM OR A BUR-DENSOME CHOICE. How can we accept the existence of the Object? We debate between applying theory to architecture as objects in their own right as well as self-repercussions of architectural inhab-itation. Existentially, we start to identify that perhaps our archi-tecture feels aban-donment, where we do not guide and orient them in their context or devel-

opment of self. But if we ourselves are also objects then is architecture not also responsible for its own actions?

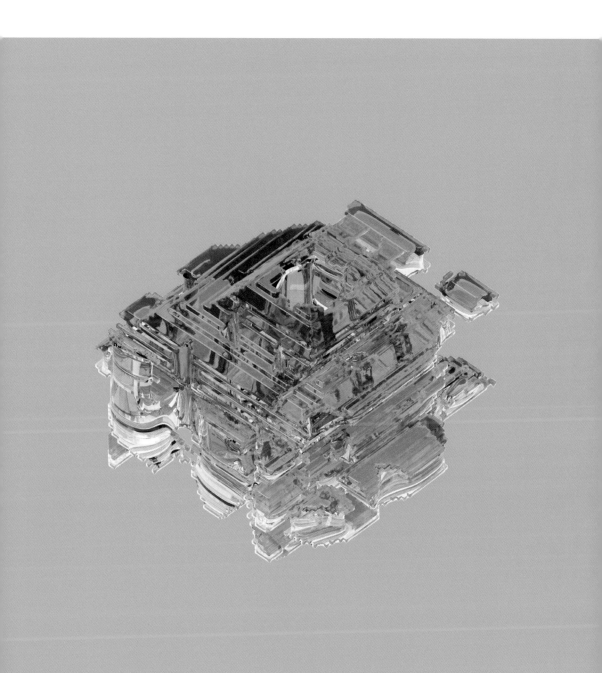

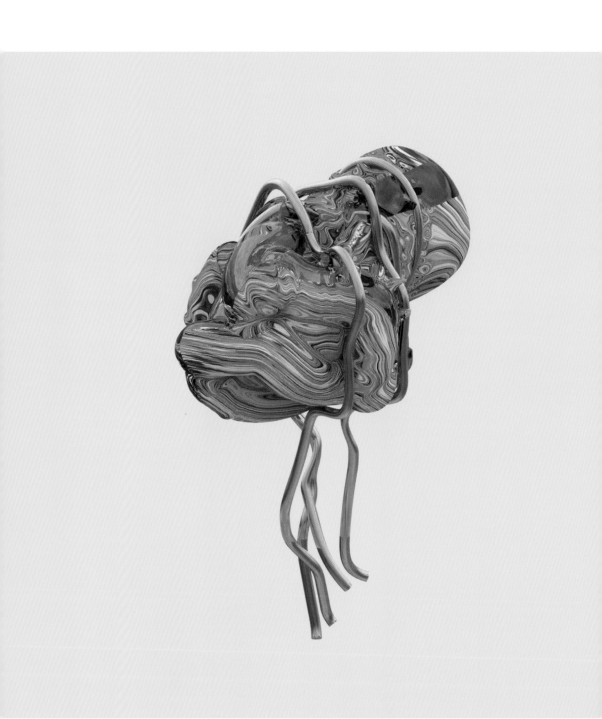

ARCHITECTURAL MYTHOLOGY.

Can architecture embrace a history that does not exist

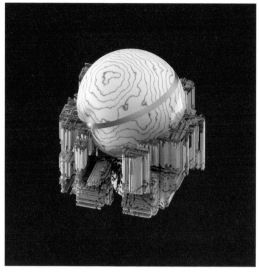

ARCHITECTURAL PRIMITIVE. Do you prefer a square over esoteric object ruination? We are far beyond the period of Modernism, we have neglected the golden ratio and ideal symmetry. Greg Lynn, pushed the boundaries of fluid form — 25 years ago. It is about time we put down Maya and consider our geometrical future and what it could become. By Investing in the new paradigm of form, from the purist primitive to the juxtaposed glitch.

physically and if so, is this work serious? *John Hejduk*, in 1985 embodied narrative through his *Mask of Medusa,* where

GAME OF LIFE. How can biological self-organization principles be applied throughout design? Collective patterns of motion found in nature are often based on relatively straightforward rules related to surrounding agents within a whole system. From such simplistic rules, an extraordinarily high level of diversity, of fractal densities and swarm configurations can be generated. However, if such mechanics could be applied to architecture as movements through systems of space, ideas and behaviors — then they could serve as a basis for development of artificial intelligence in design.

the architecture, beyond their object-like qualities, embraced a language that propelled architecture into a realm of the unknown. A realm where poetry and storytelling was as much architecture as if it was as a physical structure. Yet often architects question whether architecture truly exists beyond a few projects within the built environment. How do we decipher architecture from building? Architecture manifests itself not simply as built or even digital structure but as a narrative of thought. Therefore, mythological architectural thought might well be more architectural than the space you occupy currently.

ENVISIONING THE IDEAL. What is the importance of *The Ideal*? Plato indicates *the importance of visualizing the ideal is to understand the present*. Helping us grasp the current situation from a critical point of view, where we can understand our flaws and weaknesses in order to improve our world. Speaking of *The Form*, Plato envisions a set of instructions, a guide to an ideal image. Does architecture demand *The Form*? We vividly embellish *The Form* to the extent it becomes pastiche. We do think there is value in pursuing a common manifesto, but we reject *The Form (Ideal)*.

A NEW OPTIMISM. Can Architectural Objects, again, revive a playfulness which our discipline has lost? As architecture becomes more focused on efficiency and optimization, we often place functionality at the expense of expressionist spatial design. Movements like Postmodernism sought to return these qualities to architecture, although they did so without a strong encompassing theoretical framework — ultimately most objects were short lived. It remains to be seen if an era of objects will persist...

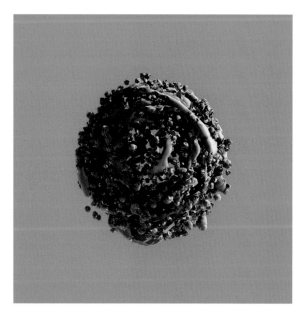

PROJECTION. Can exploring the *"fake"* help us navigate towards a deeper *real?* Invisible properties come to mind. We feel that the object itself and the underlying qualities that make it can manifest a developed nature in which to give an object meaning. Not only through its material properties but more so its geometric properties and those

MACHINE VISION. Is it right to take inspiration from a machine? Shouldn't design be more human-oriented, rather than replicating the vision of and through technology? We should be more cautious concerning the merging of technologies through designs. There is often a great risk in misplacing our priorities and designing architecture for machines or even worse enabling architecture for the worship of technology — soon to be outdated — rather than people. We should remember to step back from our computer screens and virtual simulations to take a fresh look at the world and remember who the prime user is. Are they still prime?

readable through it. Taking for instance silhouettes and projections, we can embed a nature and a language upon the object,

ORNAMENTAL ARCHITEC-TURE. Have computers destroyed the romanticism of ornamentation or revitalized it? Ornamentation is a crime in Modern architecture. With our current access to technologies we have reached a new type of ornamented surface creation, where in a matter of seconds you can generate a new pattern, color combination, a new tattoo to overlay upon the object. It is a natural desire we regularly resist, a childhood ambition, to scribble over a wall, giving it texture, giving it depth. We insist, ornamentation enhances the Architectural Object, and we embrace beauty as well as we encourage the strange — going beyond simple notions of *form follow function.*

which, in turn, is so inherently of itself, that it reveals a new real from something that did not *"exist."*

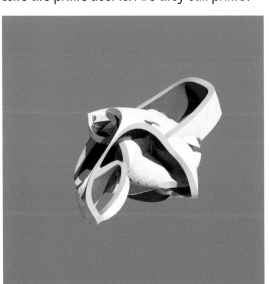

Obj. 89—91

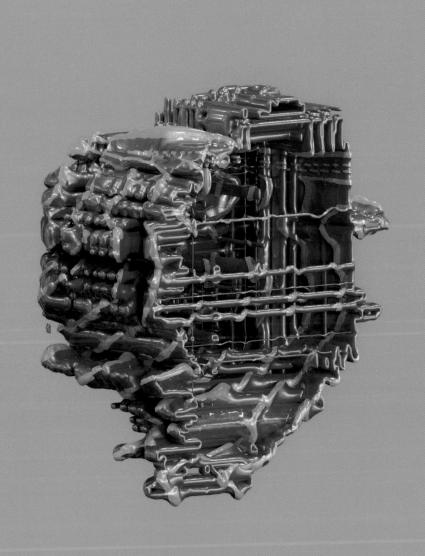

Obj. 92–182
An Act of
Submission.

Architectural restraint compresses each Architectural Object, obligating it to engage with realism while mediating abstraction. Horizontality, verticality and monumentality are negotiated with specific regards to scale and construction through the introduction of new architectural shackles. An abstracted plane forces the Architectural Objects to confer with the ground, creating juxtaposition and dilemma between the forms and an endless platonic solid. Human scale is made explicit with use, spatiality and narrative inferred by action and composition of each figure. Lastly, the gradient facilitates and expresses a wider breadth of architectural discourse, yet signifies its strangulation as it submits to a range, frozen, between zero and one.

OUT OF DATE

iheartblob

What we design today is out of date. This essay you're reading is out of date. The world is traversing along divergent paths at an incomprehensible rate; it's time Architecture started catching up. We are no longer purely physical. We live in a post-digital hybridization that is both simultaneously simulacra and tangible. Digital sensorium is so entwined within our everyday consciousness that we are often unable to decipher its impact upon society, politics and culture. And yet, architecture remains rooted in archaic traditions of static two-dimensional representations of space, and deluded hierarchies of master builders. Architecture willfully ignores the hyperstimulation that comes from its post-digital surroundings – chaotic, messy and erratic – terminology it does not wish to acknowledge as it would require fundamentally new tools, new visual languages, new methods of distribution and new theories. Its paralysis is evident in its perpetual frustration; racism, terrorism, gender inequality, sexuality and conformity all consumed daily, hourly or even every second in the form of low-res Internet images and tweets. Architecture is drowning in a slowly draining pool of Deleuzian pastiche to thunderous self-aggrandizing applause.

Blatant ignorance of these new modalities of society reflect an architecture not consumed by crisis but one finding comfort in endless apathy. We must acknowledge and embrace the fragmented and ephemeral nature of society as it is to forge a new path for Architecture. To achieve novelty and to remain relevant. Architecture does have the capability to utilize this crisis to reassert its role as a vanguard for developing critical thought through formal manifestation. However, to do so, architecture must face its abject rejection of cultural context and it must understand itself as both physical structure and digital representation in order to develop links and pathways of interwoven technologies, aesthetics and theories. Tracing intrinsic attachments between everything that Architecture encompasses: theory, tool, physical, digital, distribution and consumption.

New tools of both formal attribution and distribution leave traces of new visual dialects. When society and architecture can no longer be segregated between digital simulation and physical reality, then architecture will be liberated from its historical constraints and its own disciplinary shackles. Architecture must reclaim taboo terminology, re-investigate tropes of movement and orientation through the lens of mixed realities, articulation and form. Its role as the physical canvas between new spatial generators like AR/XR/VR must be configured and embraced not neglected.

Architecture distribution and ingestion are merging – QR codes, social media posts, downloadable apps and pseudo-critical memes are the new means of orchestrating a once purely-physical entity. Each environment in which these architectures encompass heightens discontent and inability to acknowledge technology which expands its bounds. Each effect appears as a betrayal to tried and tested theoretical principles of space, yet it's apparent that this betrayal is fundamentally altering how Architectural Objects (AOs) exist and interact with the objects surrounding them. Akin to the architectural thought they embody, these distribution platforms are inherently more decentralized and open source than traditional means, and they necessitate a propelling velocity for architecture. The works' lifespan is always limited. It ceases to influence on exiting the 24-hour news cycle and it is ultimately replenished and replaced by what is more present. We ingest more architecture through our devices than in the built configurations we are enveloped by. Traditional architectural discourse has become exhausted in this cycle – architectural memes and everyday distribution accounts are becoming more prolific and critical than the rhetoric of most snail-mail prominent architectural theorists. Instead we're left with shards of disconnected, disassociated theory, philosophy and architectural content which comprises post-structuralism, object-oriented philosophy, phenomenology and everything between and beyond. Stability is neither something apparent nor warranted.

AOs now compete against breast implants, pace makers, AI marketing, #likeforlike, crowdfunding and then against themselves. All are vying for attention within a collective consciousness that has adapted to ingesting information 140 characters at a time. Architecture's strength must be its ability to expand, reconfigure, reassert and reimagine the physical world as a coherent whole from the omnipresent visual and digital kaleidoscope in which it lives. It will achieve this through the radical unification of digital – augmented – and physical – built – reality.

Architecture is the creator of links between a society propelling forward – culturally, technologically, militarily – and traditional disciplinary forms of representation; our tools are liminal scanners between the two – visual and spatial portals that reframe objects through superpositioning and lagrangian characteristics. This leaves a gap between the physical and digital, from scars to glitches that impact our understanding of embedded and transferable information. This new visual language is Architecture. Architecture is not plans or sections; Architecture is real-time interactive applications. Architecture is not printed or static vignettes; Architecture is ephemeral, viral social media posts. Architecture is not static orthographic projections; Architecture is immersive hybrid design environments. The design and thought tools of our post-digital age are Architecture and Architecture's survival.

An Act of Submission

Obj. 92

HEALTH. Can architecture contribute to the healing process? Considering the outstanding attempts to design medicating spaces through the *Maggie's Centres,* we question how much space is linked to wellbeing. We truly believe in this intrinsic link between health and architecture but not as an *'all seeing, all knowing higher power.'* We understand the limitations of architecture but also aim to always push the limits to what people believe architecture can do. It's important for us and hopefully for those involved within the field to embrace the sensual, comforting approaches made possible by understanding space. Whether it be as simple as designing a nook for you to meet them.

SACRED. Where is the distinct characteristic within spiritual architecture? It must embody a truly special ephemeral meaning. Orchestrated play of light, shadow, sound and surface may bring true enlightenment to

BE PERSONAL. If architecture is for humanity, how do we truly deal with the uniqueness of each and every individual? Utilizing advancing techniques, we can achieve mass production and mass customization simultaneously. Consider a plug-based technology, reminiscent of the 60s avant-garde - these solutions might offer a reinvigorated vision and attitude to world building. In order to approach these solutions we must realign the attitudes of property developers - building up a solid appreciation for architecture and its tie to a progressive humanity. Thus, a collective appreciation will enable all to develop constructible, playful architecture which can combat serious issues today.

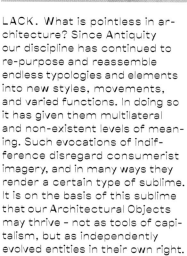

LACK. What is pointless in architecture? Since Antiquity our discipline has continued to re-purpose and reassemble endless typologies and elements into new styles, movements, and varied functions. In doing so it has given them multilateral and non-existent levels of meaning. Such evocations of indifference disregard consumerist imagery, and in many ways they render a certain type of sublime. It is on the basis of this sublime that our Architectural Objects may thrive - not as tools of capitalism, but as independently evolved entities in their own right.

those who visit. It intentionally empowers, engulfing visitors in emotive responses and heightening their level of emotive understanding, in harmony. You may contemplate, others may worship. We, as creators must remember to stay focused and really pay attention toward evoking emotion within architecture.

Obj. 93–95

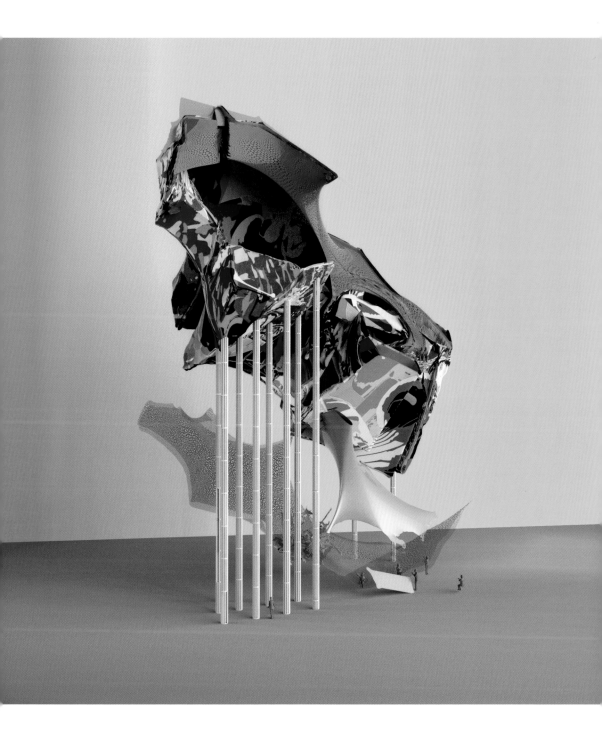

RUINATION. What really is the core essence of an object? Through ruination one will manipulate and degrade an object until only its key moments - its parti - is left intact. These moments are an expression of the object without any excess. Consider Le Corbusier's Villa Savoye within this context - we can address his core five points expressed through the Pilotis, the Free Plan, Free Facade, Ribbon Windows and the Roof Garden - they are the object without excess. However, partially, paradoxically the question of ruination indicates a relationship of parts,

MIND (IN)DEPENDENT. How do different objects influence human cognition? Our main weapon as designers, is having the power of choreographing human perception. Objects created by us shape humanities thought and subsequently define opinion surrounding them. With that in mind, our duty is to design qualities of objects carefully - as we are undoubtedly aware of their impact. The goal is to test the limit and capabilities of our objects in influencing the human psyche. Observing, analyzing how they influence the inhabitants and questioning how this may affect mainstream thought will fundamentally alter the way we shape our architecture.

ones being more important than others - its own criteria of importance comes with many faces. The core essence of an object for us lies within the realm of the partially unknown, and the speculative. Here the inability to define why, what, where and how an object is an object becomes one of the most compelling narratives of thought.

Obj. 98—100

BEYOND BINARY. How can recent advances in quantum mechanics affect our Architectural Objects? Switching our digital design from a binary system to a platform of quantum super-positioning not only presents incredible practical opportunities, but also raises massively disruptive philosophical questions. The objects we create will no longer be built with a yes or no / black or white / on or off worldview. Instead, the infinitesimal in-between may begin to be comprehensible and articulated through physical form. Such advances have even greater potential when combined with movements to create a new vocabulary of architecture built upon multiple simultaneous narratives and machine vision.

TRIAL AND ERROR. As progressive architects where do we stand in the realm of solvers and decision makers? The old guard often reject the multitude of our options, insisting that an algorithmic approach lacks authenticity because it does not involve the architect's hand. An algorithmic approach certainly does not distance the architect from their designs. Of course, a limited amount of *'control'* is given in order to solve problems of mass scale and complexity. Despite the insistence of those against the algorithmic approach - we believe that architects are connecting on a much deeper level with the machines they are working with. Beyond that of pencil and paper.

A NEW VISION. How do we move from architectural *instrument* to *apparatus*? As our current paradigm blurs the boundary between what is alive and what is machine - thereby becoming increasingly irrelevant - we must find a new common language where resemblance is no longer a dominant characteristic. We highlight quantum superpositioning - the vision of machines - as an alternative that allows us to move from indexicality to representation and representation to representational objects.

NARRATIVE. How do we fully engage with a project? One reflects on the most basic of interpretations of an architectural proposal, for instance the exposure of the parti and questions if there is another way to approach and express a project. We believe through articulate narratives architects can expose all aspects of a diversely experimental and progressive project. Expressing those

STUPID CITIES. Do we really want *smart cities*? The idea of an all-knowing, hyper-optimized grid of urbanism is in many ways enticing... Proponents trump energy-saving, commute-shortening, consumer-empowering aspects of such proposals, and yet imagining such a world seems boring, banal, and shockingly uninspired! In the same way that architecture has become a lean, efficient shell of what it once was, we risk doing the same to our urban fabric. Technology is essential to improving our cities, but we as citizens - as well as architects - must take the initiative to control how this is used through our own bottom-up initiatives and entrepreneurial ventures that strive for more than just 'smart' cities.

FORCE. Why, in the past, have totalitarian states produced monumentally progressive architecture? Consider the *Constructivist* era in Russia, this movement of progression was subsequently overturned by an equally strong reaction to control image. Architecture stands as a catalyst for control as well as prosperity. We must iterate our obsession with progression as well as collectivism. Architects have the opportunity to reject and define periods of *'time'* in concrete and steel. Don't be silenced by financial or political ambitions. You have a voice through all platforms and media - we can define our own image not solely one defined by tyranny or propaganda. nooks and crannies mostly unexplored in the mundane architectural drawings of plans and section. The narrative has become a key point of orientation in exploring and navigating the deep realm of misty architectural concepts. It can ultimately elevate a project beyond its physical stagnancy to that of story.

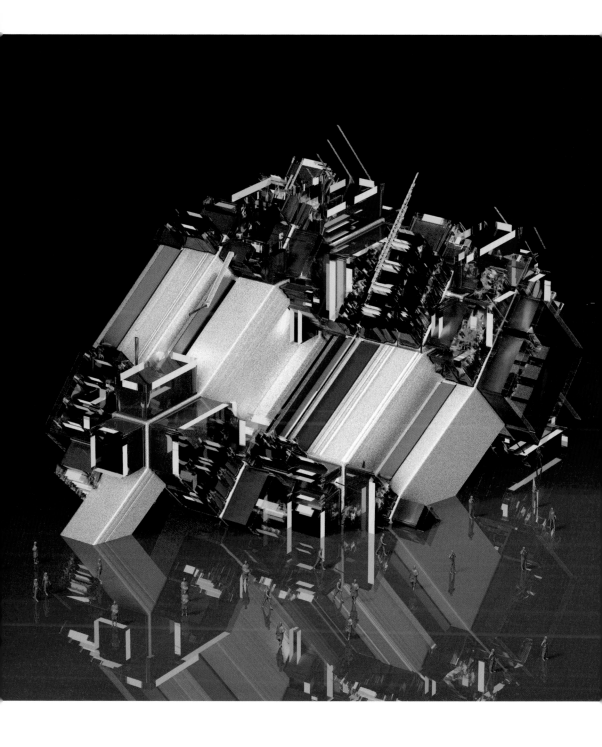

An Act of Submission

Obj. 104—105

WORLD BUILDING. How may architects engage with societal problems? Architects comment on our society through multiplicity. We may engage with near-speculative fictions in order to comment upon our current state of affairs both socio-politically and culturally. As architects we construct worlds both digitally and physically - narratively and immersively. These techniques act as a means to actively address societies questions.

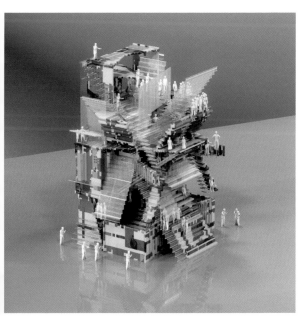

ESCHER. How does scale impact the reality of our architecture? Consider the perception of a sea from the POV of plankton and that of a whale. To one it is a viscous mass, strong, controlling and unfathomable. While to the other it is malleable, (at certain depths) confining, and (upon breach) momentarily escapable. And yet, it is still the same *real* object. When we apply such perspective to our Architectural Objects, we find that levels of fidelity and scale denote alternate spatial and sensual experiences, which fundamentally alter the perceiver's reality. Such experiences are indicative of deeper immaterial (meta) realities that exist around us, defining how we connect with form.

Something in which contractor-built masterplans and community allotments do not attempt. Fundamentally allowing architecture to thrive as the progressive thought experiment it inherently is.

CON-TAINING ARCHI-TEC-TURE.
Is it right to treat architec-ture as a

THE HYPERREAL. Why are we not honest to ourselves anymore? According to *Baudrillard's* thesis, the Hyperreal is *"more real than real."* When something fake becomes the image of reality, we must question our values. Where do these fallacies reside? In high fashion, news, social networks, the image and Disneyland. These idealized realities are determining the way we think. Imprinting unachievable expectations - leaving us longing for fulfillment that does not exist. We must stay true. Deny their façade. We must face our raw and ugly reality. Embrace it.

piece of exclusive art, available to only a few?
We think architecture always needs to be there, for everyone, taking in consideration its wider context and the population it represents. We want it to be public! Usable by any layer of society. Where there is no class separation. Let's avoid elitism in architecture - providing equal opportunities and solutions for everyone. Let's avoid privilege. Let's rethink the idea of architecture as a profession where it is built for all by all, and stands as a concrete form of societal collectivism.

NOT FOR HUMANS. How do objects exist? Human-centric design argues that objects exist in physical form for human inhabitation or human use. However, objects as theoretical, conceptual and digital ideas push beyond. Designers often place their heart and soul into creation and this is often reflected through the embracing of phenomenological human experience. Objects question their own state, neither over or undermined without sets of integral parts. These intangible beings provoke and challenge our status as human-objects within a world with sensory limitations.

Obj. 106—108

ATMOSPHERES. In what way do we experience objects? Atmospheres define the space between objects and their context, possibly creating emotional moments in time. Architects claim to be in control of atmospheres, whilst having the audacity to present two-dimensional representations devoid of our understood spatiality. Our discourse often denies atmosphere that lives beyond the stagnating use of 2D representation. We must move beyond bland black and white drawings, which fundamentally demonstrate our lack of exploration of atmosphere. We must, if we are to truly represent atmosphere, engage in exploration of spatial conditions, challenge technology and new mediums that will allow us to truly harness emotional atmospheres possessed by objects.

SEMANTICS. How can architecture span language? Jacques Derrida suggested that our experience is *linguistically mediated*; language segments can be seen as a continuously fragmented experience, which assigns meaning with each seg-<u>ment.</u> [5] Therefore, it is possible, in some sense that each linguistic culture lives within their own world. In the same fashion, our architecture today is regularly built upon progressively through the differentiation of simple computer syntax, in which some movements attempt to endow with meaning. If we instead understand meaning in the sense not that it possesses signification (*Parametricism 2.0*), but rather because of the significance of its content (or lack thereof) then we can draw from such parallels a charge for architecture which focuses not on its formation but on what it essentially is.

HOMESICK. In a world so fleeting how do we regain the feeling of home? People tend to have emotional attachment to place, especially their childhood homes. Color, pattern and image surely isn't enough. We must embellish the idea of home – with the added difficulty that we are at a point wherein 'home' may travel with us. Location will no longer be our burden, a sense of loss won't be felt - instead we shall transport the idea of home with us. We are dealing with multiple open-ended situations both socially and architecturally where we must harness emotive responses in architecture, not as a relic but as a core element within.

"There is no outside-text."
(Derrida, Jacques)

HUMAN MACHINES. Where do we see humanity within a machine-oriented future? Repetitive and programmable jobs have already been engulfed by efficient machines. More complicated disciplines such as medicine are soon to follow suit. Artificial Intelligence is benefiting our society in many ways. However, it conjures questions regarding the role of humanity within a world where machines may produce art, architecture, literature and music. If machine labor replaces human labor, our species may ultimately be freed from all relative notions of economy. Humanity may have the choice to either state their hierarchy, or ultimately we shall consume and be relegated from existence.

CUTENESS IN ARCHITECTURE. What is a real about the ideal? *Cuteness* is the opposite of serious; and yet in architecture it somehow reflects the gravity of issues our profession deals with through acting as a foil to the normal desaturated stark realism of empty renders - or worse, structures. *'Formalism'* is now considered taboo in architecture. Through Cuteness we can bring it back into our discourse - forcing architects to consider the playful, kitsch, and delightful aspects of architecture, whilst, at the same time helping to broaden the audience of architecture through education.

Obj. 114

REAL. How can architects combat the tenuous definition of the real? By placing the Architectural Object alongside technology, nature and politics one can define the Architectural Object as an equal stakeholder in the act of socio-political creation. Assuming architecture is a fact - i.e. something that is real in one way or another - then one has the ability to manipulate the truth in which architecture resides and tell its story in any order. Architecture must redefine the definition of real, from drawing to world building - we are realistic, in a world where the inexpensive banal currently exists as its only definition.

(IN) TIME. Does architecture rely upon time? Our discourse has always had ties linking political, cultural and technological progress within society. Influential linkage between these sources has directly inspired movements and style throughout the ages. Nonetheless, an object simply does not require the fourth dimension (time), to exist. However, this does not mean that it cannot act upon/within time. The object exists before its physical inception, thus it could interact (or not) at moments past, present, future or within alternate realities. Objects need not reflect their cultural, social surroundings with any regards to the fourth dimension but they must be true to themselves, no matter their context or concept of time.

DOMINO(S) AND PIZZA HUT. Is OOO Communist? It's important to distinguish between a flat ontology as a guiding philosophical principle versus a theory of value such as *commodity fetishism*. We believe the essence of our Architectural Objects exists independent of the networks and social constructs with which they are rooted. Contrast this against *Karl Marx's* argument in *Das Kapital* that a product has value in itself beyond the labor of its production, which is not a anti-realist philosophical claim. Distinguishing between reality and value creates separate lenses through which we can understand space and form. Using these frameworks to think and re-think creatively as well as conceptually furthers our discipline when done in an open yet provocative way.

BREAK IT. Is nothing new? In our age, it is difficult to articulate truly original architectural thought. While technology offers innovation to many related fields including engineering, product design and computer science - it also reflects how reliant our discipline's creativity is upon others. With this in mind, we do not criticize Brunelleschi's use of the Roman pilaster - instead, we take inspiration from the implemented use of another knowledge set. Within the context of oversimplified and compartmentalized design the use of knowledge across disciplines is too easily forgotten. Standing on the shoulders of giants like "Parametricism and post-structuralism," we cannot let that stifle our creativity as we both learn from and face these *giants* head on. By questioning architecture's intellectual assumptions, we will build radically new Objects and spaces of multi-latent qualities.

Obj. 115–117

PATIENCE. Change within architecture is never instant. How do we engage with patience in the Architectural Avant-Garde? We live in a world where we want everything, NOW! Often the Avant-Garde is gone before anyone gets to dip their toes within the built environment. As designers of our own future, we must truly engage with those who will make our ideas a reality. Without this engagement we will be confined to renders and Instagram posts of future's past. Our current generation is skeptical, but we must take advantage of our opportunities, today!

FROM OBJECT TO SPACE. What's next? The relationship between Architectural form and the spaces they create is a sensual relationship, and the balance between solid and void often is the relational metric by which our architectural expression will be judged. As our Objects evolve, we believe it is necessary for them to expose both their interi-

ors and exteriors. Our aim is to cut through this relationship between traditionally known objects, form and space.

Obj. 118–119

WIDE ANGLE LENS. What is the role of landscape in today's design context? As architects, the idea of *tabula rasa* is alluring, yet also a fiction. In considering an Architectural Object's role, we take inspiration from ancient Greek votive reliefs to make allusions between sculpture and landscape scenery. The nature of the object is similar in that both are embedded with meaning, which gives them the benefits of evolution through narrative.

(INSERT NEW MOVEMENT HERE). Are we in a state of progress? After the intellectual integration of technology through such means as *Parametricism 2.0*. We question whether we are progressing along this path, or if we have split onto a new path, specifically one which grapples with non-parametric (or misuse of parametric) design in a post-digital$_6$ era. In this setting, Postmodernism has, almost with jest, appeared to make a revival within architectural theory: wherein architectural importance is, again, explored through the notions of an object's autonomy. Architecture must always progress, and by analyzing Postmodernism, at our current moment in time, we can aim to resolve current issues surrounding critical, theoretical

DARE. Should we disregard the pull of philosophy and aesthetics within architecture in favor of new fabrication techniques? We have come to a point in which fabrication and our fascination with it, has come to an end. No longer are the parametric tools of fabrication indicative of the quality of our architecture. Aesthetics within philosophy, lay embedded in our own assumptions and the slippery slope where our assumptions live. A point of departure from the parametric is alive in the realm of assumptions. Where, we, as architects, must utilize the abundance of aesthetic qualities we have access to, in order to enhance or estrange inhabitants to the extent that they are fundamentally altered by the architecture they inhabit. These aesthetic alterations can ultimately reconfigure or encourage the inhabitant to reassess their thoughts on their spatial condition.

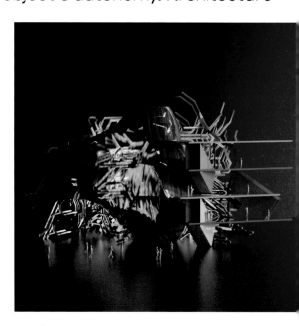

and philosophical, thought. Without establishing another movement that thoroughly embodies a pastiche or a pastiche joke.

"The term 'post-digital' can be used to describe either a contemporary disenchantment with digital information systems and media gadgets, or a period in which our fascination with these systems and gadgets has become historical" ("What Is 'Post-digital'?," Cramer, Florian)

An Act of Submission

Obj. 123–124

OLD WHITE MEN. How do we embrace architecture as a multicultural discipline? Often in academic research we find ourselves hidden behind the reality of our profession, and the old boys' clubs, which run it, alongside the elite they fondle to pay for it. We believe through technology architecture will ultimately reject, and push beyond, the hierarchical discrimination that happens throughout the profession whether it be race, sex, gender or financial status. Through the means of social media platforms alongside online crowd-sourced funding, architecture will consume the world of hashtags and online handles in order to expel the old boys' clubs and their beneficiaries from our discipline.

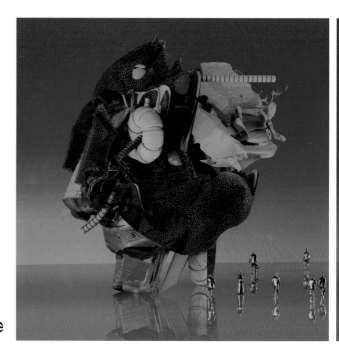

HOARDING IN ARCHITECTURE. Is this another way of allocating Objects or complete chaos? Architecture which engages with systems of instability and inconsistency may provide new models of programmatic distribution where there is room for the accidental, to blur and glitch new spatial models into inception. Through imprints of disorientation and instability one will find promise in differentiation. With new perspectives arising in the world, where we currently understand the rules that specific programmatic concerns should adhere to, we must rethink all models of spatial navigation as a way to break free from negative tendencies and predictability.

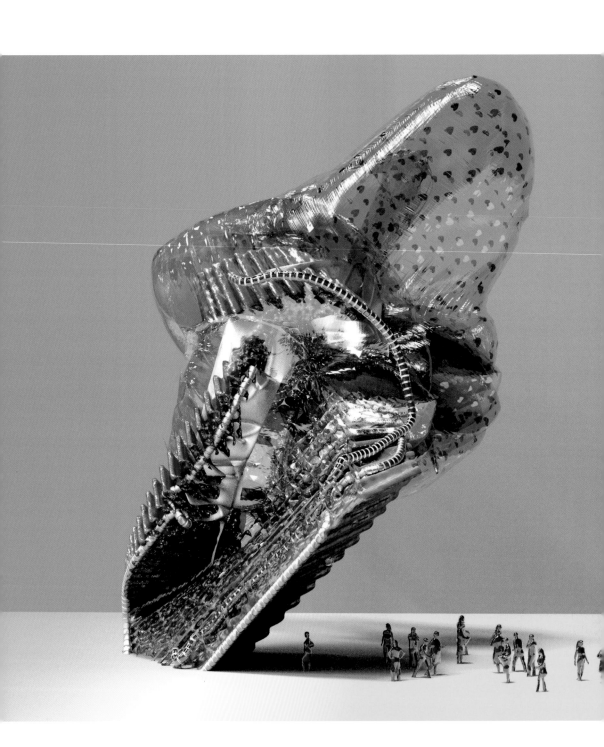

Obj. 125—127

LANGUAGE. How do we infer meaningful discussion? Bertrand *Russell*, *Ludwig Wittgenstein* and Martin *Heidegger* all agree on one thing: that *language allows comprehensive discussion*. An object in itself may be described through a multitude of adjectives, yet its inherent essence will remain stationary. Each adjective on its own requires its own thought to objectivity. The utilization of language allows for further navigation of a world wherein objects play a key role to our understanding. Without language our discussions become primitive and lose all meaning.

OUT OF BALANCE. Why embrace architecture's sensual qualities and its discrete sense of being? When space is pushed far from equilibrium, creativity takes over. This notion is explained throughout nomadic vs. sedentary space and empirically exemplified within Thermodynamics. What if our architecture has the ability to generate such singularities without equilibrium? If our architecture would matter through new forms of metaphysical interactions - conceptual breaking points. We believe these can be found in discrete object juxtapositions.

MONSTROUS DUALISM. How does one argue for the importance of the grotesque? Too often we forget that architecture is not about the ideal. It is the new real. To achieve a new idea of beauty, we must embrace a multitude of ugliness. It is imperative not to erase but embrace conflict - our generation is too quick to block, unfollow, those we don't agree with. Consider two opposing materials. Two conflicting conditions. Two rivalling textures. Argumentative forms. Bickering spatial configurations. A polemic political environment. To preserve the scars of these monsters, we can further trigger tension and create new concepts of beauty through exposing ourselves to what we are uncomfortable with; the grotesque.

ARCHITECTURAL SPEED. How does architecture respond to speed? Ultimately architecture utilizes speed to manipulate human movement. Through the use of elongated vertical ascension, architecture can manipulate and direct. Pause and declare distinguished discrete moments. As architects our interest in speed revolves around the deployment of movement as well as its control, to engender mood and vision whilst depicting nuanced space. Today, movement not only revolves around the human but also the movement of machines and their data.

One finds importance in the questioning of speed within architecture as a motive

POST-RATIONALIZATION. What comes first, *The Theory* or *The Blob*? We champion the idea of drawing conclusions through observations as a reasonable aspect both of the design process and a way through which we gain deeper philosophical understanding of form. By way of contrast, the connotation of '*post-rationalization*,' holds such negative stigmatism within our discourse - that it is often hidden behind more obscene falsehoods. Recent debates with Sanford Kwinter, give credence to the idea that our sensory perceptions of an object are equally valid pre- and post-creation. We believe that it is important to embrace the theoretical underpinnings of our designs, even those expressed subconsciously without underestimating an emotional response.

of dissecting space and controlling how humans, machines and data, as well as other more static Objects, traverse the architectural landscape.

JAPANESE PEACHES. What is kinky in architecture? Norman Foster's sex toys are buildings, but he denies it. Modernism was marketed through *Playboy* magazines in the 60s, reciprocity is now. *Just do it* says Nike and every porn video was shot on that chair - you know the one. In a world of over-stimulation it is *hard* to remain relevant yet permanent. Let us embrace architecture's ephemeral qualities. Let's all gangbang Rem in 1970.

Obj. 130

IMAGE ADDICTION. How much power does the image contain? The culture of writing has been replaced by that of the image. We are obsessed. Like junkies craving

our fix. However, the image precedes the reality it represents. The real and the imaginary, blend. Here it becomes difficult to determine the separation.

HIERARCHY OF ELEMENTS. What plays the biggest role in creating a space? Form, materiality and texture; they do not necessarily relate to each other. However, each influences the presence of object and space. Each of them can be honest but also lie, this cohesion builds tension within the architecture. One considers texture as the most influential with the power of creating illusion, form and density. Yet, we must design with distinction. We must create tension, contrasts and embrace sensorial feelings. Embed deep textures, sensual materiality, disorientating forms, distorting our understanding of reality.

LOOP. Can we really design with a sporadic, almost irrational feedback loop? Learning from machine vision has become a staple, it stands as a core element in our robotic future. Feeding physical information through machines eyes back to the physical and then, once again, toward the digital. This has become an experimental practice wherein we design with machines in mind as we explore undiscovered parameters of our own reality. Our excitement comes from the glitches, errors, flaws and obscurities developed through this transitional process.

tion. With this in mind, undoubtedly, reality is a pale, washed-out version of the image. As designers, we must take control of image-related content. We must be responsible for those we produce. Our images must inspire.

FLATTENED DICHOTOMY. Is our apparent importance a fallacy? *Timothy Morton* expresses "what we thought was special about humans is actually incredibly cheap." Herein, we must accept or at least acknowledge humanities arrogance. As architects and designers we must move beyond the realm of egotistical anthropocentric architecture and envision an architecture where there is a flattened dichotomy. Objects have always been equal yet on an opposite footing alongside our egotistical selves.

IN THE HEAT OF THE MOMENT. Should emotions be controlled and calculated in architecture? Those more knowledgeable of parametric modeling and its precision, that comes baked within it, may oppose the view that you are capable of having an emotional response from design. Others may argue that an emotional response can be parameterized down to some simple instructions. We, however, believe in wearing our hearts upon our architectural sleeves. When designing, there should be an allowance for risk; uncomfortable positions where our methods may not be accurate or orthodox, but vie for a more divide activated response.

Obj. 134—135

An Act of Submission

MORAL. Must architects be concerned about the morality of creating a better future? One poses the thought that architecture in itself does not aim to provide definitive answers for a moral reality of our world. Nevertheless, we stand by the notion that archi-tec-ture must ques-tion for bet-ter or worse the moral fabric of our soci-

A CONCEPT FOR ART. What does art look like without humans? Despite Graham Harman's long-standing claim that objects are non-relational, he reworks and develops his ontology by speci-fying that *"art needs humans to exist."* Harman admits that the Anthropocene allows a new model of thinking when reflecting upon relationships between humans, objects and the world. We must realize that albeit object oriented, objects have relationships to each other, which influence change. As architects, we must understand our responsibility for the process-es and relationships that we ignite.

eties. As architects we should embrace that architecture is inher-ently a thought experiment. Although as a thought experiment, it does not require the same unbiased or scientific modes of ex-perimentation many disciplines expect. In many cases, its role as

a thought experiment does not necessarily manifest it-self through the form of *buildings.*

PRETTY. How does *pretty* fall within the character-istics of architecture? Through the notions of a flattened hierarchy, one re-embraces *pretty* as a serious, architectural tool. As serious as the mod-ernist notion of form follows function, as serious as *Le Corbusier's Five Points of Architecture.* It must be treated with the same respect. If not, we pigeonhole ourselves into realm of appropriate and inappropriate architectural thought, and we find ourselves back in the same lineage enforced by standard architectural academia. *"Pretty"* falls within no certain set of characteristics, its importance remains, for us, in breaking the ste-reotypical nature of architectural speech. Pulling away from spatial clichés with the ambition to discover and re-uncover a glitch in the architec-tural discourse wherein we have been inhibited by regarding architecture as pretty.

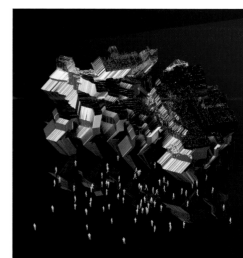

FOR SALE. Should we exploit our own? The economy of our discipline is largely fueled by built structures. Those employing experimental techniques are often seen as *unrealistic* - an inscrutable, repugnant word for David Ruy, and consequently unable to sustain large (and often small) paid workforces. The result is that we inherently undervalue our own work; whether in the form of endless competition entries or low (to non-existent) wages. Such distinctions raise issues of hierarchy and suggest we must look to new economic models for the benefit of everyone.

WITH-DRAWAL. How does the notion of with-drawal impact architecture? Discrete Architectural Objects may obtain a new lease on life, while departing from Parametric 2.0 interconnectivity. One would state that by withdrawing from correlational-based architecture we can fully embrace the design profession without prejudice. No longer should the quality of our architecture be defined through its relationship to context or the maximization of solar gain. Instead, we opt for embracing the discrete, embracing the architectural output for its inherent architectural qualities not for its effective use of reference.

Obj. 139—140

SITELESS. Does *sitelessness* devalue architectural discussion? We embolden a new way of questioning architecture, considering it as a collection of ideas or provocations. Individualized, daily concepts devoid of hypothetical site conditions encourage questions of architecture and not its correlational worth. Almost

repetitively, we iterate and reiterate our belief in the Object for its inherent quality independent of site. Architecture must pause - rethink its pedagogical values and challenge itself and its students to go beyond relational boundaries of context - whether that context be physical, theoretical or digitally inclined trends. Within this, we may liberate architectural thought and its processes from the shackles of our current architectural discourse.

FOLLIES. Why do we design objects without purpose? Referring back to the deconstructivist, Bernard Tschumi we fall back on the idea of objects without proposed function. This idea challenges the traditional core of Modernist Architecture. Providing place without function, gives the opportunity for invention, freedom and an appreciation of aura - anti-placemaking allows for complete freedom. Tschumi encouraged architecture to collide with non-architectural ideas, objects, and anti-programmed space. ₇ We encourage the embrace of this notion within our current state of architectural discourse. We want to engender conflict over resolution, fragmentation over unity, freedom over homogeneity.

AFTER. Can objects engage beyond the spectrum of this reality? Speculatively we consider our own mortality, and that of our objects, yet, often consider the thinking of *Wabi Sabi*, wherein an object which has faced its own mortality receives a new lease of life beyond its past. If so, quite practically, architecture faces its own mortality through destruction and often that of reconstitution. Thus, we believe architecture, albeit something mortal, can live multiple realities within itself. *"Is it the same Axe?"* Comes to mind.

Obj. 141—143

—————7
"The ultimate pleasure of architecture
lies in the most forbidden parts of
the architectural act; where limits are
perverted and prohibitions are trans-
gressed." (Tschumi, Bernard)

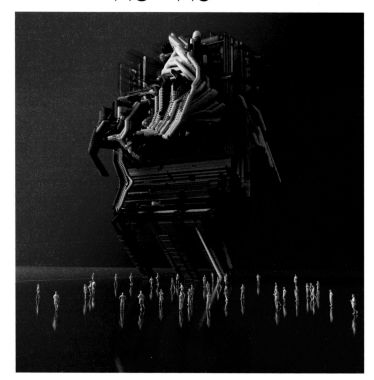

PASTICHE. How do we learn from and embrace our past without appearing pastiche? As architects we engender ideas born of precedents, yet, we must avoid stagnating in replication. If we approach precedents to extrapolate ideas and push the boundaries of what is known, tried and tested, then we will ultimately move beyond that of replication. Refrain from *Poundbury*. Refrain from what you expect. Refrain from horizontal slabs and vertical walls. Refrain from architecture. Refrain from pastiche.

TO DRAW A PLAN. Have we finally stepped beyond the plan? The plan, an archetypal architectural element limits our range of vision. Embracing the disconnect between plan, section and elevation allows to step beyond the simplicity of orthogonal extrusion. The necessity for drawing plans is obsolete, to the extent that our objects do not rely on or even stem from two-dimensional exploration.

Obj. 144—145

BIGNESS. How does scale change the inherent architectural qualities of our objects? Rem argued that *'bigness'* offered architecture the opportunity to disassociate itself from ideological and artistic movements in favor of instrumentality.[8] Nonetheless, we believe the evolutionary and sensory nature of Architectural Objects contradicts this focus on Modernist functionality. If scale elevates architecture to a distorted set of proportional relationships that unhinge it from context, then that abstraction from reality can be embraced by the object to reframe and evolve the ways we interact with space as well as with each other.

STANDING UP STRAIGHT.

What can classical structures teach us about architectural posture in a post-physical age? In our theoretical bubble of glitches, point clouds and textural imbalance, it can be refreshing to study structures more sturdy, upstanding and enduring. The work of *Karl Friedrich Schinkel* gives us tangible articulations of how modern architecture first moved from traditional rigid plans to expressive sections. It was precisely through embracing rules of proportion and scale that freedom and playfulness could be deployed. If our digital architecture is to be more than a passing fad, we must learn how to balance freedom with constraint.

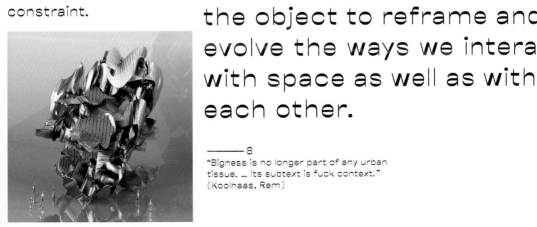

—————8
"Bigness is no longer part of any urban tissue. … Its subtext is fuck context."
(Koolhaas, Rem)

L.A. What is the difference between our perception of an object and the object itself? *Descartes* and *Locke* distinguish between the material objects of the world and the ideas by which we perceive them. However, in reality such an approach provides little reliable connection between an idea and the object(s) they represent - hence *'skepticism'* and the need for a philosophical in-between. If we instead reduce perception to its two key actors - the perceiver and the perceived - we can simplify our conclusion that the ideas we perceive are as real as their immaterial objects themselves. As architects, such a philosophical position opens new questions and possibilities for both our built structures and their digital manifestations.

Obj. 148

MIRROR. Should architecture mirror society? Complex relationships between economic exchange and power can be said to have given rise to disorientation, a key influence of *Fredric Jameson's 'Post-modernism.'* [9] That disorientation has now evolved into a level of fragmentation and polarization within our cultural modernity. Architecture needs a new formal voice to combat this growing trend, which appears only exacerbated by social media. We argue for an architecture, which attempts to recombine and collect such fragments, objects provide the transparency necessary to expose both the potential and risk such a path may offer.

TODAY. Our field moves at lightning speed along multiple trajectories, yet we often find the whole profession trundling along at a snail's pace. How can architecture truly keep up with the world it's designing for? It's a tentative question. For those clinging to a nostalgic notion of greatness, step aside. We are now also a movement of hashtags, geolocations, underground Instagram movements and the new academic. Considering this, maybe a more appropriate idea is not to drag architecture along with these movements but to shed the connotations that come with *"architecture"* itself as a profession.

—————9
In *Postmodernism, or, The Cultural Logic of Late Capitalism*, Fredric Jameson questions "...what would happen if one no longer believed in the existence of normal language, of ordinary speech, of the linguistic norm?"

EMPTY SPACES. What is the relationship between humans, machines and the spaces we inhabit together? In designing structures for both humans and inanimate objects we must switch from a traditional space-centric understanding to a surface-centric understanding of space. This accounts for the different ways we both perceive and neurally map our surroundings, as well as allows for expansion of virtual space into physical forms. From this premise, we may begin experimenting with transparency and thickness of architectural elements to embed them with meaning beyond simple dividers of social and psychological domains.

FOR US. In a moment where technology is embedded in architecture, is architecture truly embedded in society anymore? Often, architecture finds itself regarded as only for architects

WRAPPING. How do we design the interior void space against its exterior solid? As architecture becomes increasingly fluid - through the use of non-physical realities and digital tools - our forms must espouse a connection that both expands beyond building envelopes as well as integrates ideas of context and community into our architecture.

and not accessible to those who use it. With the ongoing progress of machine vision and machine learning - we are now making serious decisions wherein our architecture reflects and reacts to technology - often more than its human inhabitants. It is not difficult to envision a case where robotics have been so far embedded that you cannot distinguish the separation from architecture and technology or architecture and robotics. We must look for an architecture, which reflects this inclusion and avoids simply designing buildings for machines but instead for all, equally.

Obj. 151—153

INCOMPREHENSIBLE MEASURES. How may architects respond to scale that is not solely physical? An object contains its own physical qualities alongside human embedded relationships and functions. However, its scale metaphysically goes beyond that of physical tangibility. As architects we must attempt to grasp this almost completely intangible being. This may come in the form of an architectural narrative, wherein one can be exposed to aspects of an extended or alternative reality or through the descriptive expansion of thought concerning an object. Architecture's own stance is one mystical and murky within this *dark ecology.* [10]

PHYSICAL GLITCHES. Does perfection kill architecture? We spend so many hours trying to perfect our representational models of design. However, the most interesting moments more often than not happen through the misuse of tools, mistakes, unexpected and unexplainable errors. Whilst trying to represent our ideas, we often forget that no matter what the representation of an object is in itself an object. These representations open up infinite realms of an object, lucidly enabling readings unread and inevitably allowing projects to succeed through their misrepresentation. Embrace your diversity, the errors, the glitches, the unknown and the unexplained experiments though it's important to note not to simply aim to develop such glitches in favor of style or trend. Without these physical glitches, we may not stumble upon the unknown.

——— 10

In *Hyperobjects: Philosophy and Ecology after the End of the World*, Timothy Morton states, "For what comes into view for humans at this moment is precisely the end of the world, brought about by the encroachment of hyper-objects, one of which is assuredly Earth itself, and its geological cycles demand a geo-philosophy that doesn't think simply in terms of human events and human significance."

AMAZON PRIME. What does it mean for architecture? *Amazon* is fundamentally monopolizing all fields from drone delivery to Whole Foods and changing the entire concept of how we shop. [11] Hassle-free shopping. Ordering your groceries through your phone assistant. Simplification of the shopping experience might eventually lead us to the point in which we are purchasing architecture online. Fabrication tools, along with AI assistants, will provide, 6 Minute Abs (or 6 Minute Architecture). Architecture would be slapped with a 50% discount on *Black Friday* and free next day delivery for every *Prime Member*. This could ultimately devalue our profession to the point of sheer generic consumerism - we've already begun by configuring our home decor online. Its only saving grace may be that architecture could reach beyond the 1% who can afford it.

NATURE. Does nature appreciate architecture? Often our ruins are overgrown and taken back by nature. [12] Instead of waiting for our architecture's gloomy end in ruin we must design with nature's consumption in mind. Incorporating sensorial growth with equal footing to humans as well as machines. We must flatten the current hierarchy, wherein architecture is only for humans and consider machines and nature as equal stakeholders within any architectural project.

INFORMATION TRANSFER. How does architecture communicate? An object's constant state of proliferation and evolution - bolstered by technological innovation - causes non-conformity with traditional constructs of information sharing - e.g. centralized/unified models espoused by architects in the late 1990s and early 2000s. Instead, it is the fragmented aspects of information technology, which create both the biggest risks and opportunities for a system of machine learning paired with Architectural Objects. This coupled with new emergent visual languages of architecture will expose - and explain - us to alternate perspectives of '*reality*'; let us be cautious to not become too dependent or attached to our sentient structures, and forget about each other...

Obj. 156—158

"Our vision is to be earth's most cus-
tomer-centric company; to build a place
where people can come to find and
discover anything they might want to buy
online." (Amazon mission statement)

"The duelists knee deep in the mud.
With every move they make, they
are gradually burying themselves
together. How quickly depends on how
aggressive they are … The belligerents

don't notice the abyss they're rushing
into…" (Serres, Michel, *The Natural
Contract*).

An Act of Submission

Obj. 159—161

COMPLEX LOCATION.

Where are we? *Alfred North Whitehead's* doctrine of simple location claimed a fallacy of misplaced concreteness - substituting representation for the real world. And yet, as the *real* world becomes blurred by new modes of vision, augmented interactions and digital content, perhaps we are slowly and unknowingly placing a new grid over our reality. What is real continues to be redefined. As architects this opens up new possibilities to embrace and explore how our discipline moves forward formally and philosophically.

FRINGE EFFECT.

How does superpositioning affect architectural realities and representations? Superpositioning is a key driver of new visual languages of architecture: provoking us to envision multiple aspects of an object simultaneously akin to Analytic Cubism. Formally, this disperses the delineation of an object's boundaries thereby confronting our traditional temporal notions of spatiality and thus altering our perception of the distinction between context, object and user. Further, such ambiguous realities antiquate traditional forms of representation by raising doubt as to their accuracy, and thus embolden further innovative representations creating a cyclical effect.

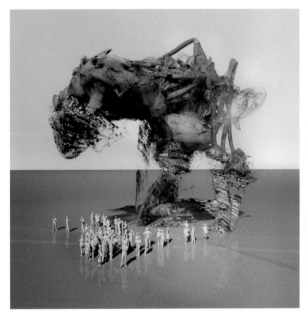

SELF REFLECTION.

What if we take a break from focusing on becoming, to enjoy what we are? Architecture is currently obsessed with its process; in academic crits as well as interviews, we discuss at length the relationships to context, parametric drivers, LEED certifications, etc. In passing we rarely mention the spatial qualities we created, an afterthought. This has smothered possibilities and ambition for true, experimental, and unpredictable architecture. In embracing our objects for what they are, we place importance where it should be on independence and meaningful architectural and spatial qualities. Those qualities which connect us as humans.

INTERLACED VISION. How can vision and the overlaying of vision contribute towards architecture? The notion of vision is purely based on who or what is viewing. Machine vision for us, allows creation of cognitive mechanisms for analytical discovery, but this is only a starting point. It must become a core ingredient in the melting pot of architectural design, pushing the boundaries of understood space. Likewise, nature's perception, or vision, of space must also be a contributing factor in a progressive design practice. Human vision, Machine vision and Sensorial growth must be utilized in a non-hierarchical fashion.

POP UP. Can architecture embrace consumerist hype culture? Like the Fidget Spinner in your pocket, architecture has the capabilities to exploit and explore the realms of the consumable. Notably, *Archizoom's No-Stop City* removes architecture from its commodity status. Similarly, we feel our objects must go beyond the icons of an economically driven culture/government, we shall never regard our architectural value through economy. Despite that, we are happy to embrace consumerist hype, fad movements and pop culture to develop architecture that may live a nomadic life, arriving and dissolving like momentary hype objects.

FORGETTING FROM LAS VEGAS. How should our objects communicate? *Robert Venturi* expressed *"architecture is not enough"* and sought to reinforce our discipline's language with explicit communication rather than subtle spatiality. However, as we enter into an era of new technologies and new realities, we argue that an Architectural Object interacts through its sensual self and need not reduce its essence to a single phrase or mode of communication. Nor should its form to be understood upon first glance.

REMNANTS. What lesson can be learnt from exploring remnants? Non-physical fragments of the past, not only whole objects, are of great significance especially those seemingly faceless ruins, which scatter the earth. A relationship between object, time and space encompasses these remnants and most human decisions will revolve around romanticizing the ruin through its cultural or historical relevance. Yet, considering these remnants not for their romantic quality but for their situation in time may become increasingly useful. Giving architects greater capabilities to challenge and situate current proposals within the 4th dimension. Considering both as primary concerns as is structure and envelope, during and after their *'decomposition'* can give us a greater understanding of its respect or disrespect for time and space.

SCHRÖDINGER'S CAT. How can architecture appreciate Schrödinger's paradox? *Erwin Schrödinger* expressed that, *if a cat were to be placed in a closed box alongside a deadly radioactive atom and if said atom decayed the cat would die.* What is important about this thought experiment is not the logistics but that the cat is in a state of multiple being. The cat is both alive and dead until the box is opened. This as a thought experiment allows architecture to utilize notions of objects that are yet to be understood, where objects may be both active and inactive simultaneously. As architects we must work within this realm of weird realism, embracing paradoxes and allowing architecture to posit notions of other worldly disposition.

Obj. 164—166

NEW MEANS OF CONTROL. When do digital systems broaden the possibilities of architecture? Digital technology allows for the integration of heterogeneous elements in unprecedented ways in the long term - but at the immediate expense of requiring architects and students to learn new languages (figurative and literal). While those who embrace such trends will push our discipline into the future, they may do so at their own expense. Without additional levels of abstraction, these new tools may currently inhibit our ability to design freely and creatively while at the same time restricting continuity of team dynamics, thereby building isolation rather than the openness they promise.

THE LIFE OF PABLO. What can OOO learn from Cubism? Cubism as an art movement sought to simultaneously portray multiple views of an object without hierarchy. This resulted in different objects states being created dis-

CORRUPTION. What can we learn from misusing digital tools? There is something sublime about the distorted glitch aesthetics produced by applications of other disciplines' tools when used for inventing architecture. Often, the performative nature of non-design tools produces interconnected spaces when applied to formal articulations through non-visual legibility and understood with phenomenal transparency. More importantly, it is through such experimentation that we become exposed to new avenues of design and new applications of architecture.

cretely yet perceptually as one. In a similar fashion, the object was painted upon a canvas' background disconnected but with an affected relationship. The movement led to new modes of vision, but rarely manifested itself in architecture. If we apply these principles to the relationship between the sensual and the real we may create Architectural Objects whose multifaceted reading is at once not fully understood or complete.

METAMORPHOSIS. What is the relationship between our unconscious and new technology-aided optics? This 19th century question, raised by *Walter Benjamin* [13], is just as satisfyingly appropriate to architecture discourse today as it was in the 19th century. Just as neo classicists struggled with the duality of legible - historic - forms vs new construction materiality and emerging mechanical perspectives, so too must we mediate between established processes of formal creation and that of new complex machine - alien - spatial interpretations. We can take inspiration from iron structures, which went through processes of hybridization, mutation and rationalization to birth the *Eiffel Tower*. Let us follow our unconscious urge to embrace a new object-oriented approach to

DASEIN. Are we able to embody *Heidegger's Dasein* through architecture? Firstly, *Martin Heidegger* dictates that *Dasein* [14] does not distinguish himself from the world in which he exists. By contrast, he comes to understand that all beings exist and equally do not exist. Most importantly, he is aware of his own existence as something to be defined by himself. If we can embody this notion through our architecture we will move beyond a relational discourse. Here / Wherein, Architectural Objects themselves define their own existence and not its *"components"* nor the public's opinion of it. Architecture must live authentically.

be better equipped to confront and repair the fragmentation taking place in our cultural modernity.

———— 13
Walter Benjamin in *The Work of Art in the Age of Mechanical Reproduction*, parallels the cameras ability to introduces us to unconscious optics as does psychoanalysis to unconscious impulses.

———— 14
Dasein, according to Heideggar in *Being and Time*, is "that entity which in its Being has this very Being as an issue."

BEYOND THE SUBLIME. Do new forms of digital art and architecture provoke a reinterpretation of traditional aesthetic theory? The philosophical notion of pleasure of perception – traditionally associated with aesthetics – has been overshadowed in architecture since the 18th century by the violent, destructive and awe-inspiring power of the sublime. However, contemporary *'cute,'* neo-spatial, digital works evoke meanings, expressions, feelings and moods through new media. These could be argued to reflect a reinterpretation of traditional aesthetic philosophy that evolve from the volcanic nature of the sublime design process itself.

WHOLE-TO-WHOLE RELATIONSHIPS. Consider Architectural Objects as discrete entities – unable to be *undermined* or *overmined* – how does that change their relationships to each other? The idea of *part-to-whole* relationships in architecture assumes a level of interconnectivity from the fundamental elements – as Rem would suggest – to an overarching role within an ecology – as LEED certifications imply.

LOOKING VS. READING. What happens when architecture engages the mind of the viewer rather than her <u>eye?</u> [15] Within architecture this distinction could be translated as *'looking'* versus *'reading'* of an object. When we design for an object to be looked at we place focus on an anthropocentric oriented idea of vision, with materiality and surfaces playing key roles. However, if we place importance on reading, then the fusion of temporal and spatial factors becomes increasingly relevant – similarly to that a Cubist painting uses intersecting, overlapping, and interlocking objects to create fluctuating configurations.

However, these ideas degrade our complex, time-consuming, expensive structures into a mere set of justifications, often represented by a simple flow arrow diagram. If we embrace our works as layered multiplicities that cannot be simply understood on first glance, then their relationships to each other are also affected. Instead of considering only their parts, we examine the impact of *whole-to-whole* relationships; juxtapositions of complex beings with their in-between voids and solids often creating new types of space through intersections.

Obj. 172—174

——————15
Sol LeWitt claimed that "conceptual art
is made to engage the mind of the
viewer rather than his eye or emotions."

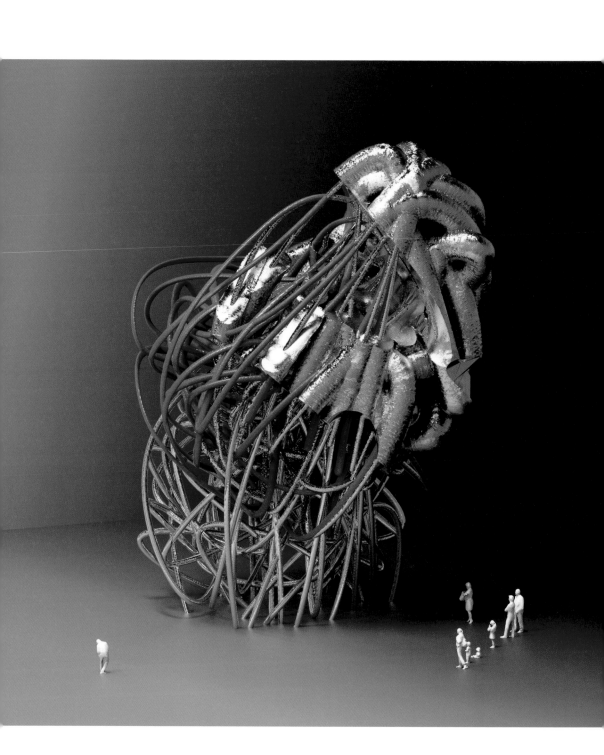

ORNAMENT. How is ornamentation defined in *current* architecture? Gothic architects celebrated ornamentation disguised through the formal aspects of structure. However, within our emerging digital design platforms whereby we're faced with multi-realities, the definition of ornament is becoming increasingly blurred. It moves toward the fluid, augmented: detached from physical geometries as well as playing roles for structural components in many agent-based systems. We can use these tools to reintroduce and challenge the idea of ornamentation within architecture. In doing some we can explore conditions of aesthetics that have been all but forgotten since Modernism took center stage.

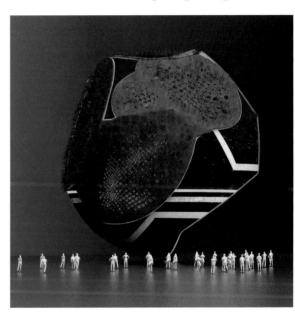

GREED. To what extent can we rely on technology? *Dr. Chloe Malevich* emphatically declared that *no ecosystem should ever perish due to the greed of a single species (Intergovernmental Panel on Climate Change Report 2011)*. And yet our urban sprawl now has spread from the Everglades to Kyoto. If - as Cedric Price would suggest - *technology is the answer*, we wonder when is the question raised? At what point do we as architects question the status quo, and react to new sustainable design and scientific processes to ensure an urbanism, which is more appropriate to future generations? Now.

SPACE TOURISM. How do we design environments to accommodate our future space population? At the moment the discussion about leaving Earth is almost fictional. However, we must discuss our wildest fantasies now and invent self-sustainable habitats to be our future homes. As architects, we should not be confined by any environment. Any atmosphere. Any gravitational pull. Instead, we must work closely with current technology and material research progressing us toward a future unknown.

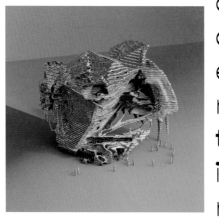

DEFY HIERARCHY. In what way can architecture approach Objects, which are equally existing but differently? We question the nature in which we utilize objects within our architecture. Whether this comes down to element or metaphysical ideology embedded within, one must openly acknowledge the equal and opposite importance of each. We must flatten our architectural, capitalistic, necessity of hierarchy. Attempting to confront these issues will undoubtedly lead to a more holistic approach to the architecture we perceive and construct.

Obj. 177—178

PROCESS OR REGRESSION.
Can we really appreciate the temporality of process? The transformation from process to outcome must be challenged as

those who stand by process-driven architecture often deny an outcome as this would result in a frozen object unaffected by its changing parameters. Information is passed back and forth until a point of equilibrium is made between process and outcome. In spite of this, we believe that the key component is not in what way form is achieved nor its contextualism, histor-

MODES.
If we saw the world through multiple guises, would a more thoughtful future succeed? We envision a world occupied by multiple modes of perception from human-centrically animated to the *vision* of inanimate objects. This embodies a nature in which we can embrace all aspects of our world through the physical and metaphysical as actors within our design process. Through the exploration of these thoughts, we will uncover new modes of experience in architecture, new modes of perception. Fully liberating ourselves from the inertly physical.

SCULPTURE.
When does sculpture become architecture and vice versa? People tend to see sculptures as works of art, whereas architecture is appropriated as functional shelter. Most, do not allow architecture the freedom of geometry and concept, in turn, they turn towards the monotonous nature of contractor-designed projects. If architecture is to succeed socially, we must praise it for what it is, art in built form. We must not simply reject a traditional view of architecture but rather firmly state it as a form of realism, which alongside technology, politics and nature can be of critical importance regarding our state of being.

icism or any other ism involved. We are engrossed by the outcome and the importance as an object in itself, void of its process or correlation. Although we understand time and process are essential, we cannot allow ourselves to fully justify the complexity of an object through that of a series of developmental steps, by doing so reduces the object into mere products of a list of instructions.

POST-PHYSICAL. Can we truly embrace the flat? Through OOO, flatness of equal existence questions our obsession with the tangible. We put so much emphasis on what we can touch that a stigma has developed feverishly toward that of the digital object. However, of course the digital object is as real as the device you view it on. We fully believe in the flattening of hierarchy and the freeing of objects from their physical shackles. [16]

Obj. 182

———— 16

Descartes expressed in Discourse on
Method; and, Meditations on First
Philosophy, *"all objects that have ever
entered my mind when awake, had
no more truth than the illusions of my
dreams."*

Obj. 183—273
An Act of Liberation.

Each Architectural Object determines its own independence from, or interdependence with, topography through constant turmoil. The transactions (rejections, integrations, reactions) created are juxtaposed and superimposed upon the endless depths of a colorless abyss ad infinitum. Each world discovering new avenues of discourse that are often exposed through their fragmented connections and ad-libs. Considered with Rebellion and Submission, Liberation is the final arc of a collaged exploration that exposes architectural thought inseparable from an object's architectural identity in order to pursue a new visual language of architecture.

ANDREW WITT

CYLINDRICAL SELF-PORTRAITS AND DEEP DREAMS: THE MEREOLOGIST'S SCRAP-BOOK

In 1970 Daniel Libeskind began a remarkable series of experiments in the structure of recombinant images. Composed of square fragments of isometric Corbusian elements shuffled in strictly gridded matrices, his "Axonometric Crystal" drawings radically reformatted classical part–whole relationships. The spliced and reassembled drawings adopted a cryptic quality of a puzzle or visual Rubix Cube (Libeskind called some "Rebuses") and the optical character of kaleidoscopic snapshots. Occasionally intercut with tabular texts, stock quotes, and other alphanumeric data, they are vertiginous oddities equidistant between constructed drawing and collage. The rigorous observance of a gridded matrix as organizing principle allows the patchwork of drawing fragments to be perceived as a coherent gesture. Each Axonometric Crystal thus became a matrix of images registering a new architectural whole.

The architectural uses of image collections have found new currency of late, not only in a resurgence of the collage aesthetic reminiscent of Libeskind's, but more critically in the technological intensification of seeing through digital image matrices that shape the symbiotic development of both human and machine perception. Regarding human perception, our intuitions of spaces, objects, and

—————1
Lorraine Daston
and Peter Galison.
Objectivity. New York:
Zone Books,
2001. P. 17.

—————2
In the Germanisches
Nationalmuseum.

ideas are increasingly informed (and collectivized) by image atlases furnished instantly by digital search engines. Individual images, regardless of quality, are no longer monadic exemplars but instead merely single constituent instances within larger collections sorted and filtered by machine intelligence. These matrices shape, perhaps decisively, the intuition of the designer. Regarding machine perception, contemporary systems of artificial intelligence are not truly independent of human judgement but are trained on vast human-categorized matrices of images. The training of neural networks is an exercise in imprinting human intuitions and associations on adaptive digital classifiers. This human-computer symbiosis of vision — humans training computers, computers training humans — depends on image databases which are comprehensive and multi-perspectival. Like the fly's eye, or Libeskind's Axonometric Crystals, our perceptions and ontologies have become photogrammetric, our new visions stitched from a shimmering mosaic of discrete image particulars.

The image matrix is a peculiar mode of both archiving and experiencing simultaneous vision. Here I will consider the image matrix as a specific medium of experience, training, and creation, and what its AI-mediated evolution portends for the future of design.

TECTONICS OF THE IMAGE MATRIX

There is a specific kind of objectivity implied by a total archive of distinct views of an object. Peter Galison and Lorraine Daston have argued: "To be objective is to aspire to knowledge that bears no trace of the knower ... objectivity is blind sight, seeing without interference, interpretation, or intelligence." [1] This is the objectivity of the image matrix: by recording a total archive of subjective views, a new total vision emerges not in any of these particulars but within the collection in aggregate.

The image matrix as a total archive has a specific lineage in visual culture which connects it to modes of recording/archiving and modes of dwelling/experiencing. The matrix is both a ledger of knowledge accounting and an entity of irreducible spatial extension. Occasionally these functions intersect, such as in the genre of the *gallery painting:* a painting which itself depicts dozens of other paintings in the context of a museum or private viewing room, a kind of painting matrix. Sometimes known as cabinet paintings or *Kunstkammer,* these recursive pictures reached the apex of their popularity in the eighteenth century. A paradigmatic example of such atlases-in-an-image is Johann Michael Bretschneider's (1680–1729) "Picture Gallery" of 1702. [2] Bretschneider presents the interior of the cavernous space,

————3
Panini was no stranger to the more typical cabinet paintings, as his 1749 "Interior of a Picture Gallery with the Collection of Cardinal Silvio Valenti Gonzaga" shows.

————4
Lorraine Daston and Peter Galison. Objectivity. New York: Zone Books, 2001. P. 122.

over 10 meters high, bounded by walls encrusted with no less than 157 paintings of every scale and description, ranging from still lifes to portraits and dramatic tableaus. The frames of these images are endlessly varying but exactly coincident, composed in an arrangement of precise geometric and thematic symmetry. Some gallery paintings directly considered the recursive structure of architectural representation. In his 1757 pair of paintings "Picture Gallery with Views of Ancient Rome" and "Picture Gallery with Views of Modern Rome," Giovanni Paolo Panini depicts voluminous neo-classical *enfilade* galleries hung with dozens of nested paintings of then-contemporary and antiquarian Roman buildings. [3] A kind of Pinterest board of enlightenment classicism, each frame is a window into a distinct vision of architecture. Panini's images are catalogs of dozens of spaces simultaneously experienced.

Mechanical means of image making such as photography inevitably intensified the recording and cataloging of images. The photographic image matrix was particularly adapted to scientific subjects, such as the biological, geological, and physical atlases and "systematic assemblages of images" that, as Dalton and Galison have observed,

shaped the notion of "mechanical objectivity." [4] When that mechanical objectivity was turned toward humans, it gave rise to the unusual genre of serialized self-portraiture, a kind of Total Selfie composed of several coordinated photographs of the subject. Consider the particular instance of the cylindrical self-portrait of Gaspard-Félix Tournachon. A pioneer of aerial photography better known pseudonymously as Nadar, Tournachon, in his cylindrical self-portait, photographed himself from a series of rotational perspectives. Like the phases of the moon, Tournachon created a serialized orbital record of his head. In principle, given sufficiently good quality of these images, it should be possible to photogrammetrically reconstruct a 3D version of Nadar from his unique self-portrait. Tournachon's portrait thus was, in effect, one of the earliest 3D scans by image matrix.

Beyond its role as a medium recording and anthologizing vision, the image matrix has more recently evolved into a medium of intensified, dynamic, and luminous visual experience. The gallery image has given way to the media-saturated sensory amplification chamber. A remarkable instance of this development is Ken Isaacs' 1962 "Knowledge Box," a media cocoon intended for inculcation through an spectacular matrix of coordinated imagery: "Inside the Knowledge Box, alone and quiet, the student would see a rapid procession of thoughts and ideas projected onto the walls, ceiling, and floor in a panoply of pictures,

———5
"The Knowledge Box."
In Life, September 14 1962.
P. 109.

———6
Victor Margolin. "Ken Isaacs: Matrix
Designer." In The Politics of the
Artificial: Essays on Design
and Design Studies.
P. 67.

———7
"The Knowledge Box." In Life,
September 14 1962. P. 110.

———8
Frank Rosenblatt. The Perceptron:
A Probabilistic Model of
Information Storage
and Organization.
In Psychological
Review, Vol. 65,
No. 6, 1958.

words, and thought patterns."[5] In his essay "Ken Isaacs: Matrix Designer," Victor Margolin describes the Knowledge Box as "a 12' square wood, Masonite, and steel cube with twenty-four projectors, including four underneath it, which cast images simultaneously onto the six surfaces that surrounded people moving freely inside it."[6] Surrounded by coordinated slide-projected screens, the user of the Knowledge Box is bathed in the mediated glow of images and data, edified by the mere experience of perception.

The contemporary endgame of the image matrix as media experience is Black Egg's 2016 installation "Social Galaxy" for Samsung's flagship New York store — a kind of Knowledge Box to the ultimate degree. Social Galaxy is a mirrored room furnished with scores of synchronized phone-sized screens. The screens extract image, video, and data content from social media feeds and display the content in this unique private theatre, but the source of the content is almost incidental to the intensity of the experience itself. A dynamic quilt of imagery, Social Galaxy partakes of the logic of filmic montage, elements juxtaposed and jostled edge to edge,

a breathing instance of a *Kunstkammer* painting.

THE EPISTEMOLOGY OF THE TRAINING SET

The intensity of an image matrix at the scale of architecture furnishes a singular experience for the human observer, whose intuition is often an intended object of training. Isaacs considered his Knowledge Box, for example, to be "a crude forerunner to a whole new mode of education"[7] made possible through the direct optical communication of knowledge. But a common neuro-mathematical model for human and computational perception of images suggests serialized image training is equally applicable to machines. The digital collation of images — in other words, the collection of training sets — is thus also a first step toward deep machine learning. The training set — a large collection of exemplars that allow a neural network to extract implied formal associations — defines implicit relationships of parts to whole not as a set of rules but as a canon of instances.

Training sets have been a fundamental feature of machine learning since the early days of Frank Rosenblatt's 1958 Perceptron, the original model of neural nets.[8] Rosenblatt called the Perceptron a "hypothetical nervous system" and distinguished his new paradigm of neurological computation from programmatic or scripted approaches

————9
Frank Rosenblatt.
The Perceptron:
A Probabilistic Model of Information
Storage and Organization.
In Psychological Review,
Vol. 65, No. 6, 1958. P. 381.

————10
Leon A. Gatys; Alexander S. Ecker;
Matthias Bethge. "Image Style Transfer Using
Convolutional Neural Networks."
In 2016 IEEE Conference on Computer Vision
and Pattern Recognition (CVPR),
June 2016, pp. 2414–2423.

————11
Caroline Preece "Google opens up
Deep Dream software, terrifies world."

————12
Andrew Witt.
"Cartogrammic Metamorphologies;
or, Enter the Rowebot."
in Log Journal of Architecture.
no. 36, Winter 2016. Cover copy.

————13
Edmund Husserl. The Shorter Logical
Investigations. International Library
of Philosophy, 2004.

even recognizable, from the training set, but they are blended and warped into unaccountable new arrangements. No mere patchworks, the sutures of training set images are seamlessly blended into new wholes.

Our office and others have trained machine-vision enabled tools to classify and dream of new assemblages and phantasmagorias of architecture from vast training image matrices. [12] Neural networks provide an eerily artful new mode of computational design, unconstrained by the explicit encoding of scripted methodologies. Machine vision and learning open the door to a new mode of meta-perception and an attendant shift in design itself.

to computation, what he called "profusion of brain models which amount simply to logical contrivances for performing particular algorithms." [9] In contrast, neural nets, deep learning, and other modes of machine intelligence approximate human judgements in the definition and application of formal rules solely from the observation of instances of that judgement. Neural nets watch and learn. New methods of style transfer based on A.I. parse implied semantic content of images, extracting and transforming features from one diagrammatic skeleton to another. [10] When turned toward the production of entirely new imagery, such as with Google's uncanny 2015 Deep Dream platform, the results have a shockingly vivid, even hallucinatory quality of recursive self-similarity. [11] Parts of the generated images may seem familiar,

THE ECSTATIC MATRIX

The rearrangement of the relationship between human, machine, and visual intuition mirrors an equally fundamental shift in the venerable relationship between parts and whole as understood in the image. In his *Logical Investigations* the logician and philosopher Edmund Husserl (1859–1938) ventures a tripartite scheme of the relationship of wholes and parts: the part, the whole, and the logical relation between the two. [13] Husserl's work was an early contribution to mereology, the branch of symbolic logic and later computer science which explicated a mathematics of parts/whole relationships. The images of our concern, by Husserl's account, have the chameleonic quality of being variously parts or wholes: an image is logically composed of sub-images, or an image may itself be part of a larger assemblage of images or more extensive process. The appearance of robust machine intelligence systems injected a new kind of parts/whole relationship mediated by transformations of perception.

In his unusual book *What Heaven Looks Like: Comments on a Strange Wordless Book,* the art theorist James Elkins provides an idiosyncratic view of one hallucinatory image matrix. He offers a tour of "fifty-two small, round watercolor paintings based on the visions [an anonymous seventeenth-century painter] saw in the ends of firewood logs." [14] Exhumed from the forgotten archives of the University of Glasgow, these enigmatic images trace a revelatory narrative in perfectly regular vignettes. Picture, if you will, this artist with the end of a log strapped to his eyes like a Microsoft Hololens, in the throes of ecstatic vision, sight bounded only by imagination. Elkins ventures a coda for this collection of paintings:

> In alchemical books
> there are pictures
> of people who walk
> without feet: they
> represent the final
> stage in the alche-
> mist's quest, when he
> is nearly fixed in place
> but still needs to move
> a bit further ... He is
> showing us something
> that we cannot copy:
> the trick of walking

———— 14
James Elkins. What Heaven Looks Like: Comments on a Strange Wordless Book. New York: Laboratory Books, 2017.

———— 15
James Elkins. What Heaven Looks Like: Comments on a Strange Wordless Book. New York: Laboratory Books, 2017. P. 108.

without feet, on threads of lightning. This is the pseudo-cosmic nature, breathing and moving, dangerous and tantalizing, immediately at hand and utterly inaccessible. [15]

What is it, today, that we cannot copy? The advent of scalable neural networks and deep learning processes imply that bots trained with human intuitions can be applied to catalog, and generatively redeploy, massive and unprecedented datasets of images — possibly *every* image. What may have once proved elusive to quantification — such as the realm of ecstatic vision — no longer seems beyond the bounds of calculation. On the contrary, we may be on the cusp of a generation of prolific hallucinatory machines — co-creators of monsters, chimeras, illusive visions of a shimmering future.

NEW CONVENTIONS, OLD PROBLEMS

KUTAN AYATA

Let's contemplate the future for a moment and accelerate a bit, play it out as far as we can to see how it might all unfold. Tricky thing to steer clear from the clichés of future predictions where technological fetish dictates all human experience; or rosy utopias where we will have steered clear of all conflicts, miraculously living in peace and harmony; or, on the totally opposite end of the scale, of optimism where total apocalyptic collapse awaits us, when our ignorance towards one another and our environment will have relegated us to driving retro-fit ATV's on desert (or water)-scapes, meandering between tips of skyscrapers which are now buried, signifying the former glory of humankind... These tropes are all too familiar, overly exhausted through our obsessive future-prediction histories, relying heavily on the advanced technology flavor of the day. One has to admit though, it is hard to avoid the temptation of technological narratives, as sometimes they are just too convenient, tempting and appear too plausible as initially considered thought experiments regarding the future reality of our world.

　　This is precisely where architecture is always stuck, operating in a perpetual misalignment of a present reality which governs its Zeitgeist and an unknown future in which architectural projections have to be eventually situated in, a future which is ever so tricky to stabilize

as a condition to speculate in. This is especially challenging in the context of this very moment of rapid technological innovation, political division, environmental decay and a culture at large whose upbringing and maturation cannot be compared to any other moment in history where new technologies and their domestication outpace our ability to analyze and diagnose their cultural consequences... If Architecture is to be reflective of its culture for which it envisions, it seems the culture it seeks to embody is in a constant state of flux and transformation, almost purposely avoiding any desire to be captured, unless of course it is on Instagram.

　　Architecture, as a built form, is a clumsy medium, especially architecture, which solely invests itself in the medium of building. Funny thing to state such distinction, but that all too famous quote by Robin Evans still rules supreme: "Architects do not make buildings, they make drawings (representations) of buildings." One could argue that the discipline of architecture operates on multiple fronts to speculate on the future reality of our environment; there are those who only believe real architecture is built architecture through professional practice; there are those who believe any built form of architecture is complicit in a system which slowly devours our resources and future; architectural production must thus be one of critique and resistance, There are those who believe in the supremacy of "paper architecture" which motivates at least a part of the architectural discipline to "practice" outside of the draconian constraints of the market place to pursue the exploration of alternative ideas regarding architecture. These constituencies who refuses to comply, to align, to be complicit with the conditions of "reality" are often the ones that open up new trajectories for architectural thinking towards alternate aesthetics and politics. The space of architectural representation is what we uniquely have as a discipline, where we can experiment without bounds, without constraints, without clients, without rules, to test the range of our imagination and discover new sensibilities.

For almost two eons, the discipline of architecture, as it developed and matured, operated through a handful of conventions to mediate architectural thought towards a future reality. While the renditions of these conventions varied from generation to generation, the principles through which they have been conceptualized remained intact. I am off course talking about the orthographic set: Plan, Section and Elevation. It has been exactly 500 years since Rafael declared in his letter to Pope Leo X the detailed descriptions of these representational conventions. To this day, this trio are still an integral part of our representational arsenal even though our mode of design fully transformed from projecting towards an architectural object through an interrelated set of generative drawings to extracting a set of drawings (almost as proof of scheme) from a digitally conceived architectural object. One might even argue that there is no need to record a plan or a section of a project in the convention of drawing, since the digital data set of the project holds all necessary information for its eventual realization. Yet, we still generate plans, we still generate sections and elevations, we still generate axonometrics in various forms. We do so to be able to discuss new architectural thinking in relative terms to the lineage of our discursive histories. Since the digital turn and post-digital twist, we have rapidly expanded how we mediate architectural thought and define new representational techniques. It is no longer viable to define a single medium as the predominant mode of representation in Architecture. The reality of our time is that we operate and move in-between multiple mediums. Just to list a few: Animations, Coding&Scripting, Figural Axonometrics, Virtual Reality Interfaces, Augmented Reality Protocols, 3D Renderings, Holograms, Digital Collage, 3D Printing, A.I., Robotics, Instagram… For a discipline which argued its ideas mostly through plans, elevations and sections up until thirty years ago, this now not-so-recent paradigm shift, which is by all measures still in its infancy, defines a unique moment within the history of our discourse. As these recently cultivated representational mediums take hold in the discipline, slowly but steadily claiming their discursive polemics, and stake their positions, they, too, will mature into "mundane" conventions. Once their novelty wears off and the foregrounding of their technology no longer provides an adequate buzz, they, too, will have to operate beyond their Zeitgeist and deal with the old problems of architecture.

To debate whether these technologies of mediation have really arrived, proven worthy or whether they will stand the test of the discipline and time, is now a foregone conclusion. There will always be those who will staunchly believe in emerging technologies to be nothing more then a tool which enable the expedient and efficient execution of architectural ideas, locating architectural thinking independently from technological development. And there will be those who will insist on the idealism of technology being at the center of human progress and seek its expression. The more interesting domain probably exists somewhere in the middle of these positions with regards to architectural representation where any medium, whether analog, digital or virtual, avoids the fetishization and stylization of their generative technologies.

Obj. 183—184

DUCKS OR DECORATED SHEDS. What else is there? Denise Scott Brown and Robert Venturi articulated an array of distinctions between *Ducks,* and *Decorated Sheds* within their seminal text, *Learning from Las Vegas* in 1972. The *Decorated Shed,* typologically stands as a structure with indicative signage of what appears beyond its doors. Embellishing the *Duck* throughout our Architectural Objects, they become their own icon – their own embodiment. Yet it is important to acknowledge our avoidance of literal symbolism. Functions are indirect, unknown and unaddressed through an expressive aesthetic language of inherent Architectural Objects. Indefinable forms which allude to a past, present and future beyond the familiarity found in cook-punch architecture though, we do not throw away vague familiarism as we accept all readings of our objects – especially those unknown to us.

GOING OUT OF BUSINESS SALE. What happens when shopping malls die? *Victor Gruen's* utopic vision for healthy social interaction manifested itself in a capitalist-driven, never-ending series of 'junk spaces.' Notoriously, since diagnosis, this disease has spread and smothered much of the public realm, and yet we are the reason, with endless consumption, we implicitly encourage such developments. Aside from economic concepts of scale and scope, they provide unique spatial conditions, often alien in their surroundings – offering escape. While better alternatives exist, they do serve as conduits of social interaction – the new *medieval streets* – which we risk losing as a result of digital marketplace juggernauts (Amazon, Alibaba) disrupt the way we purchase goods. Malls are already left abandoned, being taken over by nature, and if we are not careful we may soon find a similar fate for our physical interactions, left only with digital spaces and social media.

RESILIENCE. Shake hands. A good pat on the back. How may architecture oppose these notions of insincerity? We feel the lack of authenticity and conviction within architecture today, encouraged by a nuanced professionalism, is diminishing the sheer strength the profession could hold within the built realm. Although, we accept that no architect must be tied to a theoretical standpoint of their early twenties, we seek those with strength to reinforce their thinking even if that thinking may be overturned tomorrow. We must undoubtedly defend our thesis and not sit idle as others trod over what we believe or disbelieve. We must embrace activist notions of an architecture at war with bureaucracy. We will no longer be tied to financial gain. Instead, architecture may act as form of protest to those 'Yes men' who rule our world.

AN AMPU-TATED ARCHI-TEC-TURE. How do we heal lost limbs of a city? Cities are constantly regenerated, replacing

TURN ON YOUR HOUSE. What are the next 5 point (clouds) of architecture? Corbusier's notion of architecture as a machine for living is far more complicated in a world augmented by digital realities, machine learning algorithms and an Internet of Things. When we consider Architectural Objects as living, sensual objects whose spaces are often collections of 'machines,' then the Modernist notion will bifurcate from its part-to-whole formation into something far more spatial, interesting and relevant today. Ultimately these five points (clouds) of architecture will rely not so much on simple objects as pilotis or ribbon windows but with their navigation of Machine visibility their inherent autonomy.

old for new. Scars show like illegal surgeries, architecture is lost overnight as the *Repo Men* reclaim valuable land within the city. In some way its raw honesty and violence are its beauty. Architectural Objects act as symbiotic beings clutching at scars within the city they vie in conflict, unity and within their own ignorance. We deny the vulgar repetitive notion of pastiche, which fill gaps aiming to avoid scars on our cities like a celebrity's most recent Botox treatment. These scars remind us of who we are in a city of history of loss and embedded within a city yet to be written.

Obj. 185—187

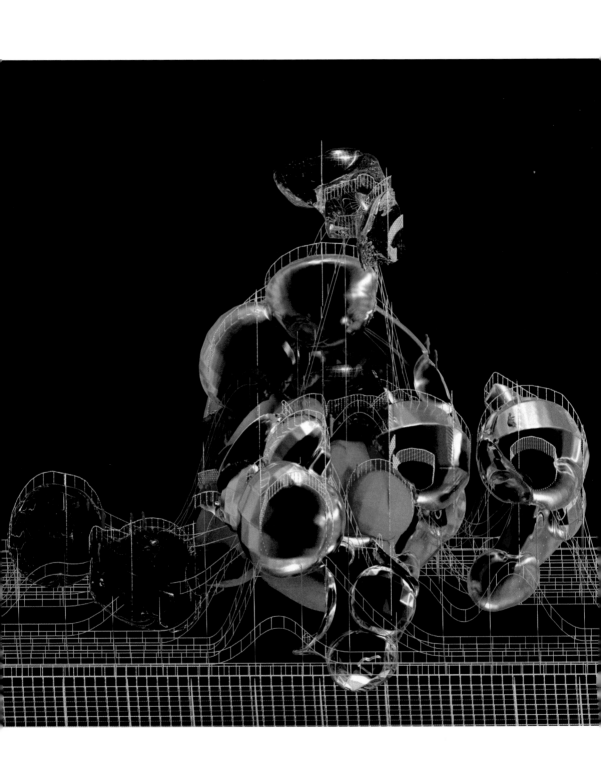

Obj. 188

ROLLER COASTER OF LOVE. Have gadgets killed architecture? Historically, experimental architecture has served as an incubator for future established *conventional* practice – a means to expose the general public to the "*Technology of the Fantastic*" as Rem described it. Conversely, we as architects somehow no longer seem to dream of alternative futures – our *experiments* are increasingly focused on efficiency, structure and control rather than *poetic technologies* furthering the individual nature of technological experience has already begun disruption on non-architectural scales. A revival of the once inspirational nature of our discipline will engender the confidence to take back our role as sculptors of our collective future. [17]

———— 17
"There is a secret shame hovering over all us in the twenty-first century" and that "the feeling is rooted in a profound sense of disappointment about the nature of the world we live in."
(Graeber, David, *The Utopia of Rules*)

INEFFABLE INFLATABLES. How do we learn from the 60s plug-ins, mega-structures and inflatables without posing another level of pastiche? To thoroughly avoid hybridization of *contemporary* and precedent motifs we must evaluate our surroundings – like the radicals who have paved the way for a succession of exper- imental schools, practices and stu- dents alike. Not direct- ly of our

BACK IN MY DAY. What did we do again? There is no unified direction for archi- tecture – Parametricism 2.0 has been the only, relatively, articulate recent at- tempt. Historians may have a hard time depicting a period of progress or uni- fied thought. Perhaps it has been *"too easy"* for our epoch. Without significant political angst in a global sense, archi- tects must group together to progress through a series of experimental pro- cesses we have not needed to address our failures. However, such current issues as: privacy, terrorism, gender identifica- tion, gender inequality and racism don't often get the attention they deserve in architecture. We ignore our cultur- al societal presence both positively and negatively in favor of efficiency. We have the tools to build tall, wide and sprawling. Now, it's time we forgot.

physical cities attributes but those concern- ing conceptual, political, application driven dystopia of the period in which we live. Un- der no circumstances do we disregard past or present – we avidly vote for a future constructed of socially activated angst, our contempt, our complacency, our happi- ness, our comfort. *"Stay calm, inhabiting is easy."*——18

Obj. 189—190

————18

Andrea Branzi, refers to the seminal work *No-Stop City, 1969-72*
by Archizoom, where the city is
an unfathomable void, yet our
apt ability to inhabit is enforced
by simple furniture which acts

as a guiding principle of living
and orientation.urniture which
acts as a guiding principle of
living and orientation.

P300. Are we necessary? *Generative Adversarial Networks (GANs)* are already learning to optimize structure, to recognize beauty and create unique imagery, leaving us as architects to worry that they may soon synergize their capabilities rendering us obsolete. How we as a profession choose to distinguish our work today will determine future jobs and the role of our discipline. The cliché that machines are

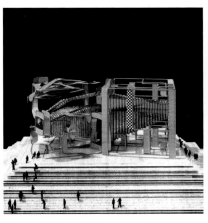

LIFELINE. Where should architecture avoid? In 1971, *Archizoom* (ironically) proposed to cover the entire surface of the earth in architecture, this forced us to question where is off limits. This issue is increasingly pertinent as seemingly anything is a potential plot. NASA's architectural competitions for the surface of Mars is a strong indicator of this. Additionally, the rise of a digital landscape further confounds the idea by suggesting that what is off limits physically may not be so digitally. The renewal of the existing, potentially through digital injections, lets objects grow and evolve across realities rather than constantly adding new carbon footprints, which are ill-equipped to survive in this era of rapid change.

APERTURE. How do we maintain meaningful perceptions within a chaotic world? *Kurt Koffka* articulated that, *"the whole is something else than the sum of its parts,"* referring to the capacity of our brain to generate continuous imagery from fragmented visual perceptions. Consciously opposing the idea that the *'whole'* is more or equal to an aggregation of its parts. Applied to our architectural organization principles, we can extrapolate this idea to further break away from Cartesian constraints, which seek to subvert freedom for diversity. Dynamic agglomerative spaces engage in mixed modes of representation, which serve as further *complete* forms of perception enabling cognitive growth within an increasingly over-saturated world.

simply tools to help us, is too vague and hollow to stand against innovations in Artificial Intelligence. Our competitive advantage as architects lies in our roles as creators of form and space. We need to show the world that architecture is not about settling for the lowest common denominator. Nor are we the interface between multiple professions. Instead, our knowledge must expand to express that our importance lies upon a complex instinctual result of innate human capabilities combined with philosophical thought and executed with a desire for novelty.

Obj. 191—193

Obj. 194–196

GET USED TO
IT. Will nature
ever accept
its emerg-
ing identity?
Global warm-
ing is often
declared as
a reaction to

GOING BACKWARDS. Why do we always
go back to the basics? Sometimes,
it feels like there is nothing more to
explore in architecture. Frequently –
instead of looking for new inspiration –
a safe way for architects to *progress*
is to search within a bank of precedent
knowledge. We however believe that
this is often a dangerous path to ven-
ture down – akin to driving your car
by only looking through the rear-view
mirror. We must pursue purpose,
goals, and undeniably our own agenda.
We do not need to always go back
to basics of form or thought for clarity.
Time and time again we must reiterate this – respect the classics. Avoid
pastiche.

human being's harmful activities on Earth; increased hurricanes,
earthquakes as well as water pollution is a direct outcome of the
culture of production, consumerism and the *necessary* waste
processes of humanity. There is so much trash on Earth, that at
some point, nature will have to adapt, as to any other constant
phenomena; it is simply in *Nature's* nature. We can only imagine
that after fighting these alien items, "trash" will become ac-
cepted as an essential part of a new biologically mutated hybridized nature. Plastic, metal, and acids may merge with organic
tissues discovering new identities for the Natural. Illustrating this

hybrid
future,
we thrive
for the
creation
of these
half-
breed
objects,
which
combine
a multi-
plicity
of quali-
ties both
natural
and
human
made.

TIME'S UP. How do we
design with time in
mind? Our cultures are
fast moving, buildings
expire every 50 years if
they're lucky (some places
have shelf lives of less
than 20). In our lifetime,
whole cities will regen-
erate and this presents
opportunity for a new
period of built experimentation. Interwoven digi-
tal/virtual, physical and
augmented space can
prevail as successor to
the eroding expired
structures. This changes
the speed of decay, with
new means of updating
structures via data
downloads and alters a
buildings 'lifetime' by
unhinging relationships
between traditional
lump-sum catalogue ar-
chitecture vs. subscrip-
tion-based models of
continuous bespoke im-
provement.

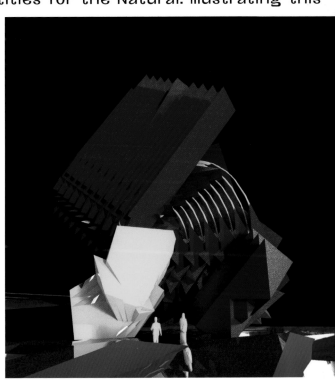

KNOW Y(OUR) PLACE. What have we learned from Postmodernism? Undoubtedly, renowned as the architecture of *pastiche,* the joke, an architecture steeped in irony and insider quips. Yet it recurs without the laughs. We encourage digital culture and all the nuances, which come with it. However, we feel obliged to articulate our concern for a world consumed by a capitalist monster, whose only driver left, appears to be in the nostalgia production industry – both socially and architecturally. If we bow down to this industry, we may find ourselves in a pseudo-Postmodernist meme. Unlike Postmodernism, the irony lies not in the cultural application of capitalism but in our absorption of capitalism as normality. At this moment, we have the world's depth of technology at our fingertips but we are consumed by the immaturity of its utilization.

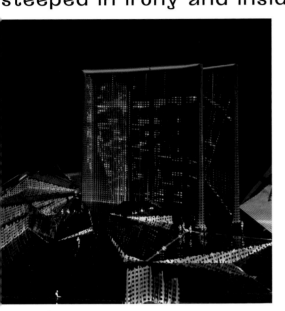

BREAK EVERYTHING. Can we transcend the physical? Deconstructivist architecture stands against the epistemic immediacy of our collective consciousness. By way of contrast, it stands bravely suggesting that everyone has an intrinsic ability to question and search for understanding through built form; in doing so, it both celebrates and undermines the very nature of the empirical. OOO can be seen as supplementing this discourse by embracing that an object's sensual nature cannot be fully described or understood. Just as Libeskind, Gehry, Tschumi as well as others pushed us to fundamentally question our physical surrounding. Balancing such notions of estrangement alongside sensual dislocation will push us to question our non-physical surroundings.

Obj. 199—201

BEAUTIFULLY DISTURBING.
How should we treat qualities that challenge the Real? As architects we can create intentional misreading perceptions through our articulation of form. Such techniques are not exclusive to our discipline: poetry and literature have often used defamiliarization (*Hemingway* and *Shklovsky* are key culprits) to create conditions in which their readers are temporarily not permitted to understand what is unravelling. In doing so the ultimate conclusion becomes all the more powerful and engulfing. Within architecture, such moments are often identified through estrangement. In our current discourse, we are freed from the shackles of process to embrace these moments in addition to delivering a stronger conceptual message, one that embraces and absorbs our impressions of associations.——19

GOLD DIGGER. Does your object have values? In the so-called *'real world,'* architecture is economically motivated with the value of objects often defined by structural efficiency, material costing and square meterage. The definition of *Building* not *Architecture* is one, which is always a cause of contention, and the tropes of both insight heated debate. Architecture will transcend beyond the core costing, m² pragmatism and evoke meaning or ask courageous questions of our discourse or simply of humanity. Theoretical ideas, concepts, aesthetics all certainly play a role in an intended response to those who inhabit, misuse and abuse the architecture unlike the practical catalogue-driven developer constructing apartment buildings designed by pseudonyms. Our interaction with Architectural Objects is intended to reach beyond basic shelter to produce memory and value; they must not be reduced to a quantifiable excel costing spreadsheet.

YOGA CLASS. Must we incorporate flexibility into architecture? In 1993, Rem celebrated flexibility through the notion of the *Typical Plan* for its calculated purity. However, today such efficient reconstructions of our spatial genealogy have led to work spaces (to name one example), which are no longer architectural; and instead are boring, capitalist and uninspired. If we contrast this against Philip Johnson's Glass House of 1949, we find an object where every detail (down to the furniture orientation) was critical to achieve a desired spatiality. What our architecture has lost is a sensory purpose – where formal elements and spatial interpretations allow us to compose our own stories rather than be told what to do. This is how we understand flexibility and you should too.

——19
"Never believe any of that about a scythe and a skull," he told her. "It [death] can be two bicycle policemen as easily, or be a bird." (Hemingway, Ernest. *The Snows of Kilimanjaro: And Other Stories.* New York: C. Scribner's Sons, 1964. Print.)

DIRTY LAUNDRY. To cure color blindness? Canonized in *Le Corbusier's Law of Ripolin*, whitewashing walls has been an architectural staple since the 1920s – still persisting within schools today. While Modernists made grand allusions of morality, health and ethics, white (more accurately, off-white) also served as a unifying formal element to a movement with varied theoretical positions. Key figures often rejected or evolved beyond such notions, including *Bruno Taut* who suggested the role of color is 'physical' and that it

NOTHING MATTERS; EVERYTHING SUCKS. [21] Does existence precede essence? Existentialism suggests an object obtains its purpose after *birth*. Architectural Objects which are not born should not and may never adhere to any set of functions, desires or requirements. An object-oriented approach argues for essence. Here objects have a life beyond physicality – one predetermined or inherent within itself. Yet instead of arguing if, one questions when essence is obtained and how much it will impact the world.

can itself be the architecture, [20] merely supported by form as evinced in his country-house in Berlin Dahlewitz. Even Le Corbusier would eventually rely heavily on color and taught that *it is part of architecture's fundamental condition*. Today color is again a topic of conversation in part due to new technological tools and access to radically shifted CMYK/RGB presets; without a well-defined conceptual stance, it may easily be re-suppressed by monochromatic simplicity for the sake of historical repetition.

―――――20
In 1919, Bruno Taut proclaimed "Color is the joy of life... since color can be given even with small means, we have to insist upon the use of color especially in times of need." (Klinkhammer, Barbara)

Obj. 202-203

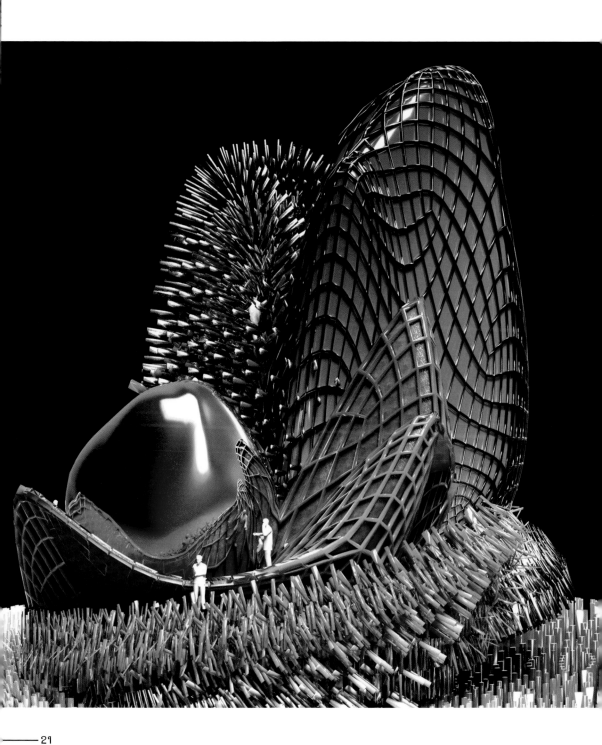

"If man as the existentialist sees him is not definable, it is because to begin with he is nothing. He will not be anything until later, and then he will be what he makes of himself. Thus, there is no human nature, because there is no God to have a conception of it. Man simply is. Not that he is simply what he conceives himself to be, but he is what he wills, and as he conceives himself after already existing – as he wills to be after that leap towards existence. Man is nothing else but that which he makes of himself. That is the first principle of existentialism." (Kaufmann, Walter)

TWO, BACK AND SIDES. Louis Kahn struggled futilely to enlist then re-enlist the strength of modernism through the monolith – purity in monumentality. Postmodernism often undercuts this notion of modernism through whimsical motifs, colorful bands and insider jokes. Aaron Betsky, exclaims that *this moment of undercutting is important in engaging the public with architecture.* It removes the stigmatic notion of elitism that follows architecture so profusely. We are happy to indulge in notions of monumentality, yet unlike post modernism we do not believe architecture should be as easily identifiably accessible as a can of Coke. The discovery of meaning plays a strong part in our Architectural Objects. Architecture is in dire need to build a bridge between the easily accessed and the theoretically esoteric. By reinterpretations, or complete redesign, of uptight white male middle class architecture – we might begin to be able to engage with diversity today.

Obj. 204

An Act of Liberation

Obj. 205—207

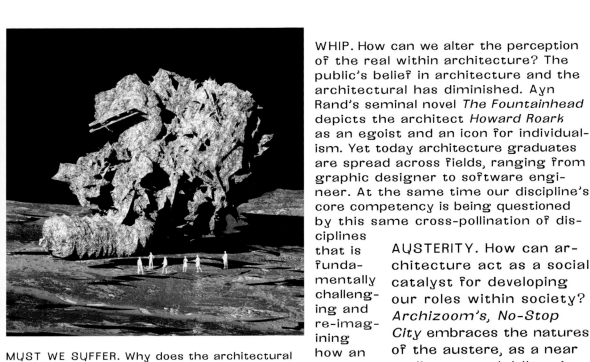

WHIP. How can we alter the perception of the real within architecture? The public's belief in architecture and the architectural has diminished. Ayn Rand's seminal novel *The Fountainhead* depicts the architect *Howard Roark* as an egoist and an icon for individualism. Yet today architecture graduates are spread across fields, ranging from graphic designer to software engineer. At the same time our discipline's core competency is being questioned by this same cross-pollination of disciplines that is fundamentally challenging and re-imagining how an architect is viewed within society today. This has the potential to reestablish our relevance or destroy it entirely. In order to enable growth

AUSTERITY. How can architecture act as a social catalyst for developing our roles within society? *Archizoom's, No-Stop City* embraces the natures of the austere, as a near endless vessel. Wherein, capitalist rhetoric is out-weighed by a multi-dimensional model of cohesion. Our link between technology and architecture is becoming ever more interconnected, through these nuanced connections – we believe architecture gains the potential to embody, all we stand for and against in the face of progress.

MUST WE SUFFER. Why does the architectural profession still exist? It has never been so unrecognizable as it is now – disregarded as an ineffective use of resources for prosperity. Development of technology has not only enhanced our abilities as designers but also further endangered our profession. The few of us left, try to keep pushing the discourse towards bigger innovative discoveries. The stereotypical idea of the architect has shifted from a well-respected individual to that of a commodity. Urban sprawl and off-the-shelf housing has invaded our cities like wildfire, they boast their poor *layouts* as if they were gifted by Vitruvius himself. This lull within architectural discovery and lack of respect gives our generation the necessary incentive to push the boundaries of the profession. It allows us to redefine what we want architecture to be and how our society must move toward a more prosperous future.

and the re-branding of the architect, we must consider an architecture which is multi-faceted, that challenges our perception of reality, wherein, one must question the very fundamentals of how we can live and the spaces (real and augmented) that facilitate that.

SENTIMENTAL. Should we value history in architecture? Restoration of dilapidated architecture often causes major damage of cultural heritage within communities. By plastering cracks, pressure washing graffiti, and removing small imperfections we often obscure momentary and interminable history, and thereby erase a valuable part of architecture's collective memory. Yet, wiping down historical scars of catastrophe is often regarded as a way to move forward. We collectively encourage the censorship of our history. Humanity chooses to remember nothing or only the good through the architecture we preserve. Instead what if we let our Architectural Objects stand as testimony to their time; to those who have visited; to those who have caused catastrophic scars,

ARCHITECTURE PARLANTE. Should architecture express use? *Oikema, Claude-Nicolas Ledoux's 1789 House of Pleasures* phallic object affirms itself in all its glory, as a fellow of function follows form – it itself is a 18th century brothel. Like our Postmodernist counterparts, objects become image and image becomes object. We feel strongly about the navigation of object and image, billboard, home, the intersection of capital and lower-case. We imagine a house tattooed in advertisements, similarly to cars which race NASCAR. The inverse is as important, for instance – a billboard which depicts a home which actually sells Coca-Cola – the advertisement itself is a double bluff. The literal translation of function following form once held great strength. However, we find value in everyday object intersections and inversions where homes and billboards exchange languages with kettles and teapots.

wounds and beautiful imperfections. Architecture can be a blank canvas, which witnesses and collects an imprint of our collective history instead of redefining the past through distortion. Do not allow those to dictate what we should and should not remember. Architecture can articulate our present through its history.

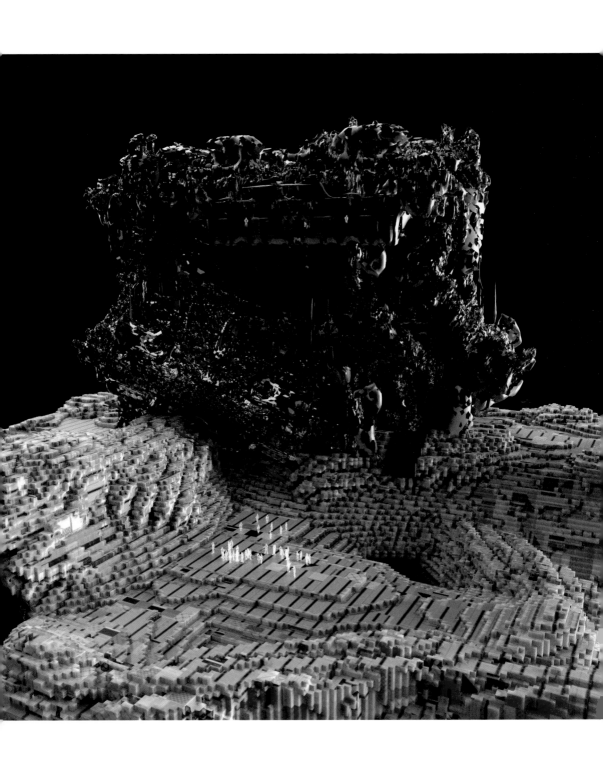

Obj. 210–212

MIDLIFE CRISIS. Experiment or build – why not both? Our discipline's use of perception is highly fragmented: from glitched interpretations of computational code – *Op Art* – to new modalities of vision through hyper-realistic vignettes. Nevertheless, these digital representations contrast heavily when standing before and against a built work of architecture. Likewise, our Architectural Objects have the ability to remain autonomous whilst acquiring new possibilities and potentials. So too should we consider how architectural perception can evolve and grow to distil meaning through built physical form.

PROMISCUOUS PATTERNS. Why should Architectural Objects (AOs) sleep around? Greg Lynn's embryological studies showed the benefits of monogamy – AOs dating within the same type can lead to interesting mutations and iterations. However, if AOs are more curious, kinky perhaps, they may begin to have sensual relationships with others outside their definable type. The resulting vastness of their experience will become a subconscious context that is embraced through its endless diversity, rather than an indexical exploration.

YRTSUDNI. Is anything really sustainable? From petri dish grown meat houses of Terreform ONE to fleshy flowers from Heide Hatry, the combination of synthetic biology, ecology and architecture is already creating new mutants, challenging the ontological boundaries of architecture and raise questions of sustainability. Such advances evoke Le Corbusier's statement that the new materials of urbanism will consist of *sky, space, trees, steel and cement in that order,* signifying an emphasis on the natural relationship between the structured world we live in and the raw concealing earth it is composed of. We advocate that Architectural Objects must sensually exist within the physical world not via LEED certifications, but rather through ontic evolutions that acknowledge and symbolize the complexity of our reality.

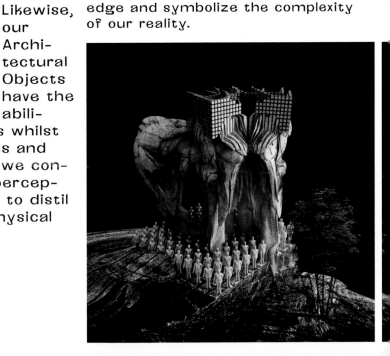

A CLASSICAL FORAY. How do we approach a period of societal (urban) trauma? *Lebbeus Woods, War and Architecture* articulates itself as a set of guiding principles for how we as architects may approach abhorrent acts upon society. We must embrace societal change, for good or for bad, embracing the nuances of our past, present and future. Quickly, after a period of crisis we resort to *"getting back to normal,"* this must be avoided – it is detrimental to our progress. If we try to replicate or simply replace architecture tarnished by brutes we will ultimately find ourselves in a setting we do not associate with or a city filled with brochure architecture born from a molten acontextual capitalist cauldron. Architectural Objects must embrace their past, present and their future by baring their scars as tokens of their history and their contribution to the society they uphold through built form. We must always reflect on the past, build on the torn and embrace the hybrid society that is born.

REAL AND *REALLY* REAL. What is the bottom line of these definitions? All objects equally exist, but they do not exist equally. A flat ontology does not claim that objects are the same; individual objects have their own essence, structure and unique qualities. Fictional and real might have the same influential power but navigate alternate meanings. An object, which exists fictionally would have a separate influence on the world, rather than an object which exists physically, showcasing its essence in the (real) reality. Whether our Architectural Objects exist virtually, theoretically, or within another dimension, they all equally exist. That being reiterated, they all exist independently with different kinds of casual powers. It is up to us as creators to identify physical and conceptual manifestations of objects to be exposed to the world.

Obj. 213—214

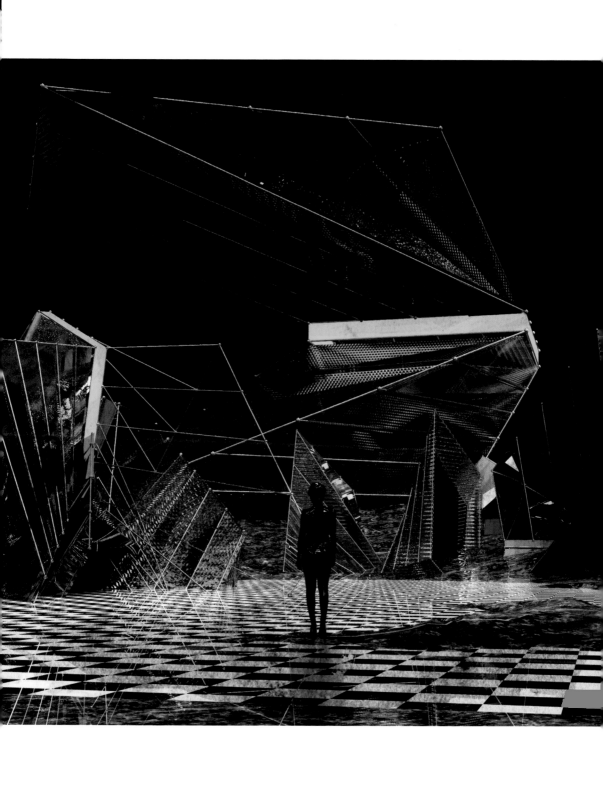

BOUNDLESS PRECEDENTS. What is context? Architects frequently and quite literally regard context as their site surroundings, with those less literal regarding it as an object situated within space and time. For example, an architecture embedded within culture both of context and of time. One questions the notion of context and whether this is important physically or at all. Considering the notion of context is a top-down process, by practicing as such, we are allowing our senses to be pushed under the rug. An Architectural Object removed from literal context may embody a more thorough contextual approach through its situation within global discourse or within a strain of thinking or feeling. We fully believe in a sensual, emotional response to architecture as a valid approach to both design and the appreciation of objects.

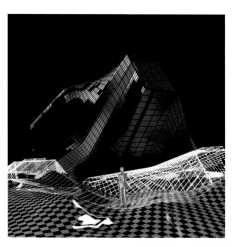

I NEEDED COLOR. [22] Can color fit with architecture's rhetoric? Color is architecture's unwanted loiterer, branded as premature, lacking elegance and overall just abhorrent in the eyes of true architects. Jim Carrey's recent artistic exploits engender painful emotion throughout expressive color – not too dissimilar to expressionist work. Color embraces presence, and lack thereof. Architecture must proceed from its snobbery, from its *old boys' club* history and instead become consumed by all that does not fit its (modernist) manifesto. Each architecture school of thought must move past their differences into a world wherein exuberant architects are not snubbed for lacking *class* or *formal*

IDEAS LEFT BEHIND. What is your intention? It does not take long to learn and understand how to detail and fit out a bathroom. It is technical. Follow the instructions and you will be fine. Our approach will never focus on technicalities. We must stop designing architecture as if it were an orthopedic reclining chair for the elderly. Albeit important, practical, technical design knowledge must be overshadowed by emotion, color and conceptual ambition. An architect should be a dreamer, irrational, enabled by their unwillingness to conform. Ideas must not be left behind, because, *your kids would love them.* We must enable a movement of architecture wherein we as architects encourage an environment populated with the estranged, the sublime and the beautiful.

decorum. Color must be embraced on multiple levels in multiple scales – from pure emotion to a subconscious psychological embrace.

—————22
"Polychromy is as powerful an
architectural tool as the plan and
section." (Le Corbusier)

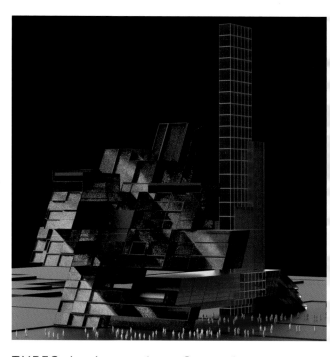

UNIVERSAL DESIGN. Is architecture accessible for everyone? In a world of Google-Earth vacations, VR weddings and drone delivery systems, barriers to experience architecture are not so much eroding as they are fundamentally changing. Removing physicality means an Expo in Kazakhstan isn't a problem for those with the right bandwidth, but does the immensity of the sphere (with its cracked glass) really translate through two-dimensional representations? One problem architects face in our current epoch is to elevate *digital architecture* beyond the screen toward experientially encaptivating space. It is an issue of both authenticity and validity when compared to the alternative of photo-

TYPES. Is the notion of typology an endangered artifact? The notion of purpose-built architecture and the lack of flexibility that indexes its existence comes and goes from the original utilization of town halls to the seminary. If the notion of type is constantly in flux, its lack of stability makes one question whether type is necessary at all. Perhaps it is nothing other than an anthropocentric fabrication for semantic categorization. We feel, the notion of type is something unsettling, something that may not even exist, and if it does in fact exist, it does not live within the banal realm in which we have confined it today, within the confines of programmatic categorization. ——23

graphic reproduction, which brings forth aspects of an Architectural Object which are unattainable to the eye (e.g. enlargement, HDR, slow motion). Ultimately one approach bridges the physical and the digital while the other separates them.

Obj. 218–219

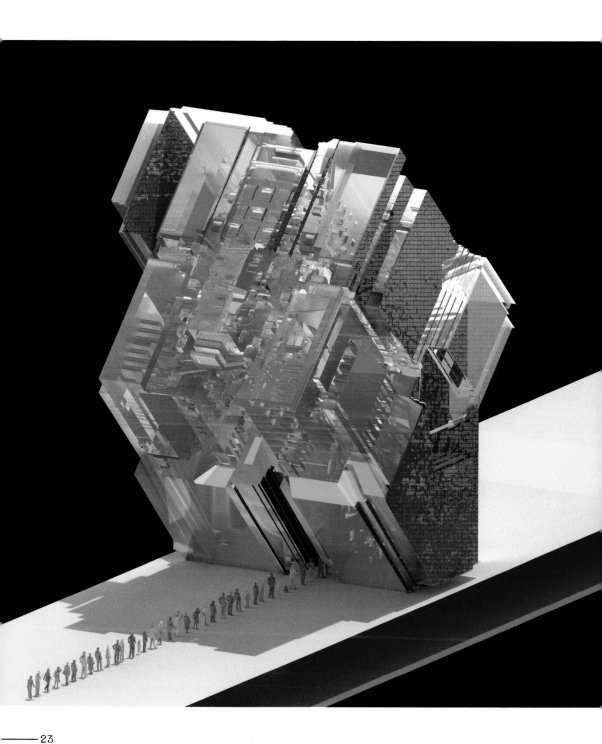

—— 23

"Junkspace is the sum total of our current architecture: we have built more than all previous history together, but we hardly register on the same scales. ... It substitutes accumulation for hierarchy, ad-

dition for composition. More and more, more is more. Junkspace is overripe and undernourishing at the same time, a colossal security blanket that covers the earth. ... Junkspace is like being condemned

to a perpetual Jacuzzi with millions of your best friends."
(Koolhaas, Rem, "Junkspace," 2006)

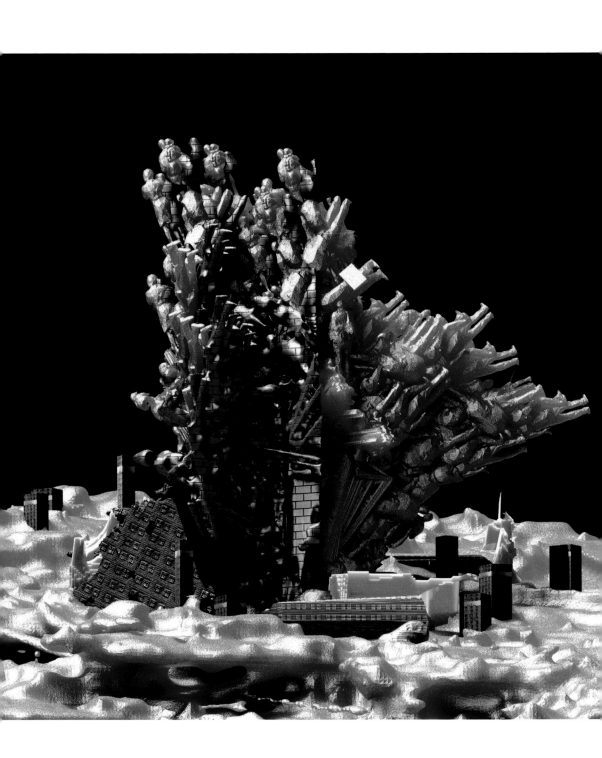

MULTIVERSE. What if our reality was exponentially weirder than we can imagine? French philosopher, Quentin Meillassoux suggests that the laws of nature can change at any given time – with no explanation. [24] Therefore, we may well be expecting a virtual god who shall appear in the future consuming the very essence of our reality. Realism tries to express that *thing*s are highly articulable objects, which may turn upon us at any time without notice. Each object may be a source of concern for a realist as they reflect on the possible world evil. Evaluation is based on all possible out-

AESTHETICS SOLD SEPARATELY. Focus on 'what' not 'why'? The elevation of architectural process has been championed by post-structuralism as a means to empower the political impact on our built environment. Yet from such laudable ambition it has often detrimentally impacted architecture as a validation/justification of its inputs with form, color and space as mere byproducts. This discounts the overwhelming impact aesthetics can have – both positively and negatively – as influencers of these exact relationships. These mere byproducts are reactionary with each other, and our Architectural Objects and may act with ferocity upon our political structures. As French philosopher, *Jacques Rancière* suggest, aesthetics has the ability to redistribute the sensible and therefore it can assert equality in ways far more directly powerful than the esoteric processes embodied in our discipline.

DISCURSIVE. How should we speak? In our world of over-stimulation and instantaneous nothings (notifications), attention has become an increasingly rare commodity. Scott Brown and Venturi's '*Decorated shed*' suggested that architecture must shout louder to be heard. However, with today's digital inputs it is advertisers such as Facebook and Google that mine our attention through OLED screens. It is easy, in the face of these new confrontations for us to retreat to historic forms of representation, arrogantly exclaiming that a clear figure ground and a compelling section will convince the public as they similarly convince our peers. Instead, our discipline must embrace the struggle, incorporate new modalities of communication (AR/VR, super-positioning, games, etc.) and let new forms of representation drive innovations within designs. If embracing it now seems like a stretch, in five years the gulf will be far too deep to cross.

comes over time yet Speculative Realism must remove correlational factors from the equation and take each object for its individual qualities – not those given to it by counterparts or outlying forces. If we begin to evaluate this we will pull out unique qualities and conditions of objects beyond their physical or metaphysical relations and ultimately reprogramming how we engage with the world.

———— 24
Quentin Meillassoux rejects correlationism: "the idea according to which we only ever have access to the correlation between thinking and being, and never to either term considered apart from the other." According to Graham Harman this restricts the philosophical understanding of being with thought by disavoing any reality external to this correlation as inaccessible, and, in this way, fails to escape the ontological reification of human experience.

SO-SO. [25] Is every Architectural Object (AO) the same? Joseph Campbell's, *Hero With a Thousand Faces*, as a comparative mythology finds similarity across all stories: secular to religious (architectural to non). The descent and return of an AO between an ordinary (real) and special (sensual) world should result in a cyclical journey of its human users between the conscious and unconscious, order and chaos, even life and death. This is the story of all great architecture from *Imhotep* to *Zaha Hadid.* [26] As architects we should not despair at the Sisyphean task this suggests, but rather embrace the absurd and defiantly (although joyfully) continue to explore meaning within architecture through discourse and the stories we tell.

Obj. 223

—————25

According to Albert Camus there is an absurdity in the human condition which constantly seeks out meaning in a world devoid of meaning, and the only way to become truly free is to embrace this absurdity.

—————26

Imhotep, known for his stepped Pyramid of Djoser 2670-2650 BC and Zaha Hadid designed her own stepped pyramid - King Abdullah Petroleum Studies and Research Centre 2017 AD.

JEVONS PARADOX. What is *Tintoretto* doing in your dining room? Architecture via digital tooling has unprecedented opportunity to control precision – be it scripted algorithmic steps or augmented construction efficiencies. This has given rise to a re-devotion of context (and anything else that can be quantified) via *Patrik Schumacher* and *Parametricism 2.0* in an exceptionally banal way. *Slavoj Žižek* notes *the safest way to ruin a piece of work is to finish it* (imagine V*enus de Milo* with both arms and a full color palette), and in many ways the suppression of spontaneity within our discipline is doing exactly that. We should try designing with computers that have more Africa in them. —27

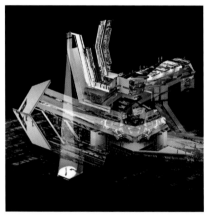

WE'RE WATCHING YOU. Why did you clear your browser history if you have nothing to hide? We live in an intensely digital society; the proliferation of smart phones, drones, Photoshop, machine learning, robotic animals and satellites means that surveillance and digital voyeurism is an established fact of life. We have internalized this reality to the point that that we no longer distinguish between what we see with our eyes and what we see through our lens. And yet, the architecture we create is often banal. Archaic. Regressive. While architecture need not mirror the reality in which we live – it should not blindly ignore that the world is moving beyond its nostalgic heritage into a new visual realm encompassing aesthetics and a morally grey era.

Obj. 224–225

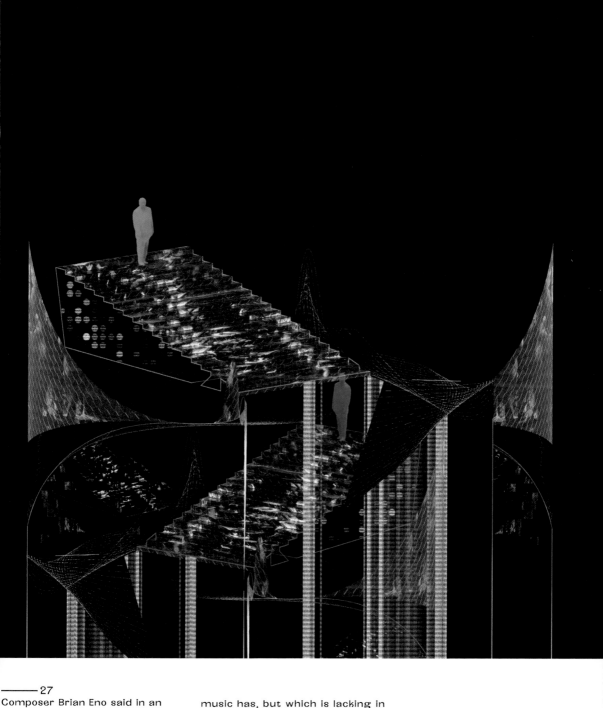

Composer Brian Eno said in an interview in 2010 'the problem with computers is that there is not enough Africa in them' referring to the peculiar and exciting mixes of sounds that African music has, but which is lacking in Western music.

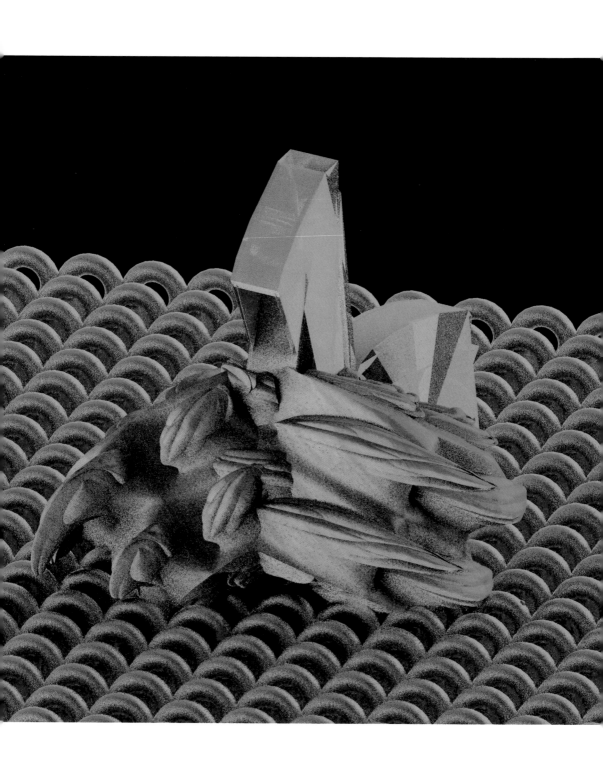

AWKWARD. Why must we avoid the awkward? This condition should not be perceived as something negative or unwanted. It is an alternative to the *normal* (average). Awkward situations develop in themselves strange objects, strange moments and unforgettable, well, awkwardness... It makes their moment in time special. It draws our attention back to their quirky being, it makes them intriguing. Let's embrace the awkward, the bizarre, the weird and the strange objects that scare you, make you uncomfortable and those which provoke your response. For if we embrace these characteristics of objects we may derive new moments, undiscoverable by being polite.

SHIFTED TALES. There is an economic dream of capital, wherein a *laissez-faire* attitude would allow those who work for it, to have their very own piece of the pie. If you don't have your slice yet then you better *pull yourself up by your bootstraps.* However, where are these bootstraps on Architectural Objects (AOs)? The opening up of the global economy has also expanded the influence of AOs. China and India present us with new cultural dilemmas in which raising ones status in society may come from a different aesthetic presence and deal differently with social inequality. The pairing of a *Global Localization* alongside *Local Globalization* will allow architects the ability to empower capital-driven and capital-starved economies, in a way which confronts negative norms without imposing foreign belief systems.

THE *GREEN* STUFF. Want to make your building sustainable? Put a tree on it! Or even better yet, add hundreds! Global warming concerns and a focus on architecture's environmental impact have sparked a pseudo-environmental solution. This *solution* has been covering heavy carbon footprints with summer coats of grass, dozens of bushes and unrealistically large trees on façade renders. It is time to stop! This pretentious, obnoxious attitude is humiliating and degrading the intelligence within the profession by suggesting we are unable to accurately understand complexity. Architecture does not need to have a tree on it to compensate its dreadful carbon footprint. Instead we must invest in the research of material and fabrication techniques, finding new ways of counteracting problems rather than wasting time duping councils into *environmentally friendly architecture* with Photoshop-applied greenery.

THE IMAGINEER. Will estrangement transform architecture? Once our thinking turns to pure practicality the craving for enigmatic space diminishes. Moments of estrangement will challenge how we act, move, inhabit, see and fundamentally challenge the purpose of architecture. Ultimately finding pressure points – where objects are pliably rigid – the many mysterious moments in-between as well as those yet to be discovered. By encouraging chal-

DENSE HISTORICISM. Can we incorporate shards of our architectural past in a densely fragmented future? *The Ningbo Historic Museum from Wang Shu and Lu Wenyu* negotiates a bridge between historical culturalism and recent conceptual thought. Here the amalgamation of materials and form coexist within a frame of historical thinking, and contribute not to the past but to the development of a future. The language of *fragmentation* is used in this context not as a term of disconnection but instead to embrace and encourage an object's individual unique qualities. We are growing more fragmented; socially, culturally, politically – through gender and race we must embrace all of the notions of individuality in favor of a global coagulated pot of collective architecture. Our Architectural Objects must therein speak to all factors of life within this world, enabling – enchanting diversity.

lenging spaces and the redefinition of architecture we attempt to flatten hierarchical jargon-ization, hopefully without appearing cliché; there are clearly no correct/incorrect spatial negotiations. If space itself can force humanity to question how we inhabit, then we can be challenged to sincerely question the tried and tested tropes of shelter and fundamentally question living. Rest assured it is more than a shifted slanted wall.

ECOLOGICAL STRUG-GLE. How can we understand the built vs. the unbuilt in today's technological climate? The controversy of ecology in architecture is not a recent phenomenon. Ecology has been at times, an enemy, an ally, a scapegoat and a catalyst for our discipline, yet throughout these roles a primary focus has been on how ecological conditions relate to and reflect upon humanity's life. Now as humanity's perceptions of reality are changing so are our relationships with the unbuilt. *Georges Leclerc Buffon's* concept that organisms and their surrounding environments are in constant struggle which leads to growth, adaptation and change may no long-

THE PRINCE AND THE IMPOSTER. Are architects *trivializing* their work through notions of fad? For instance, we believe that a nostalgia aesthetic has engulfed our society, from Arizona Iced Tea to Yung Lean, we are consumed by nostalgic rhetoric. Similarly, our architecture is currently consumed by an object revival wherein we seek comforting embrace in the utilization of found elements, platonics and color. These notions of fad are far more embedded than many are willing to accept. They may act as a way to appropriate and comment on society. However, our Architectural Objects do not aim to embrace nor reject the fad, nor do they decline their DMs. Instead our Architectural Objects embrace all moments of life and death as well as all possible realities in which our current nostalgic objects were never viral. This is a *Trivial Pursuit*.

er be so applicable in a world of mixed realities. The focus should become how our Architectural Objects struggle against their surroundings rather than the people they hold.

Obj. 231—232

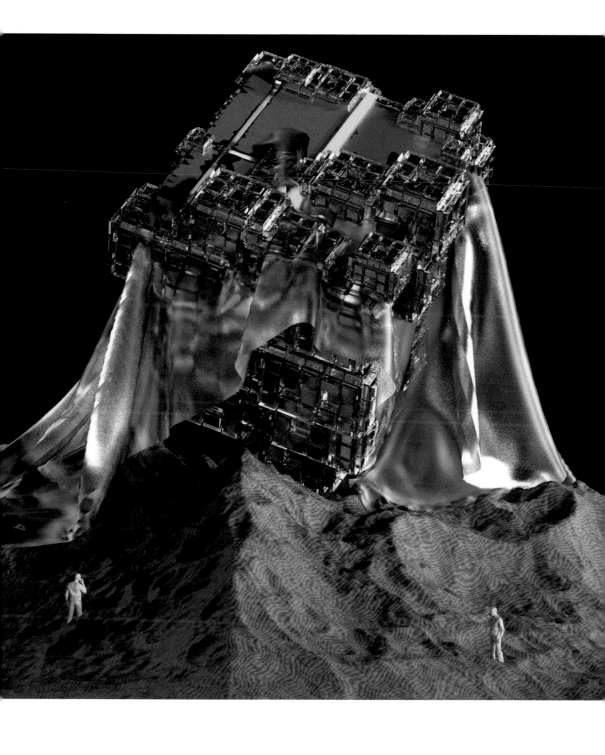

UNCONSCIOUS EXISTENCE. Does architecture need human beings? Architecture is commonly perceived as a discipline progressively sheltering humanity aligned with theoretical, historical thought. It's about time we removed the outdated notion of correlationism from French philosopher Quentin Meillassoux. Correlationism promotes a world that simply does not exist without humanity. Graham Harman often argues for a world that ultimately functions without the thoughts of humanity as the crux which makes and breaks our world as we know it. We identify with a world that also exists without our interference. This world sits separately untouched by human thought, uninfested by the anthropocene. Here objects exist simply beyond humanities knowledge – human beings ourselves, objects, are only a small part of this world in which we simply cannot understand. Architectural Objects may

ASSEMBLAGE. Should we embrace the notion of the assemblage? Each piece of architecture may be read as a consistent assemblage of objects; a symbiosis of objects and their relationships. A primary product may be a totalizing form. In order to design more balanced whole objects it is also critical to account for whole-to-whole relationships with-in the composition. Instead of each part being reliant upon its relationship to the whole, each object could act upon each other independently without their relationship to another being their defining feature.

COMING SOON. How do traditional notions of architectural context affect an Architectural Object (AO)? Assuming our AOs interact with each other, their surroundings and the existing urban realities through indirect, sensual notions, this prompts connections of space and form rather than linearity, heritage and pragmatism. Current architectural discourse lacks investigation of manifestations, which regard physical proximities, on a formal and object-like approach, not simply through material adjacency – aiming simply to blend in.

be physical through human interference, but their existence is not dependent on us. We are the transitional tool from metaphysical existence toward physical reality and our reading of them are only part of what they may be.

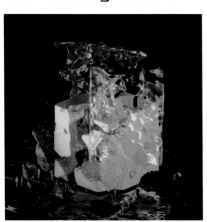

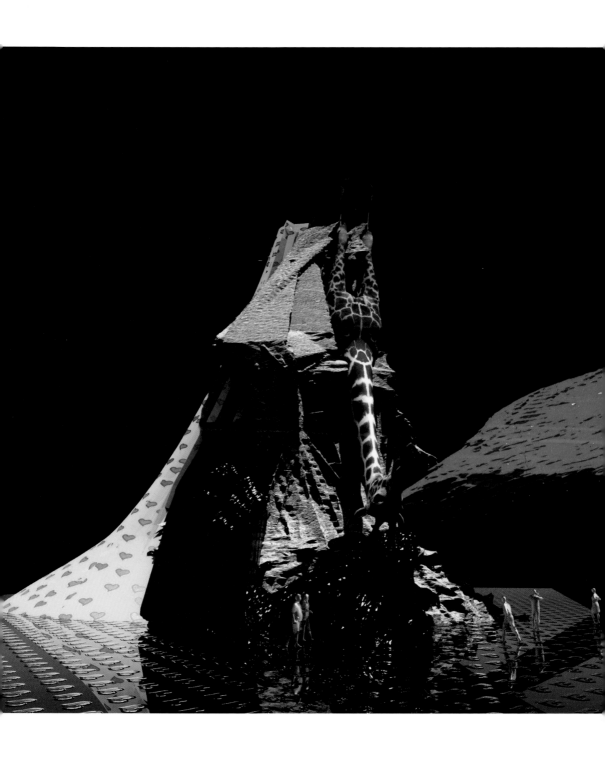

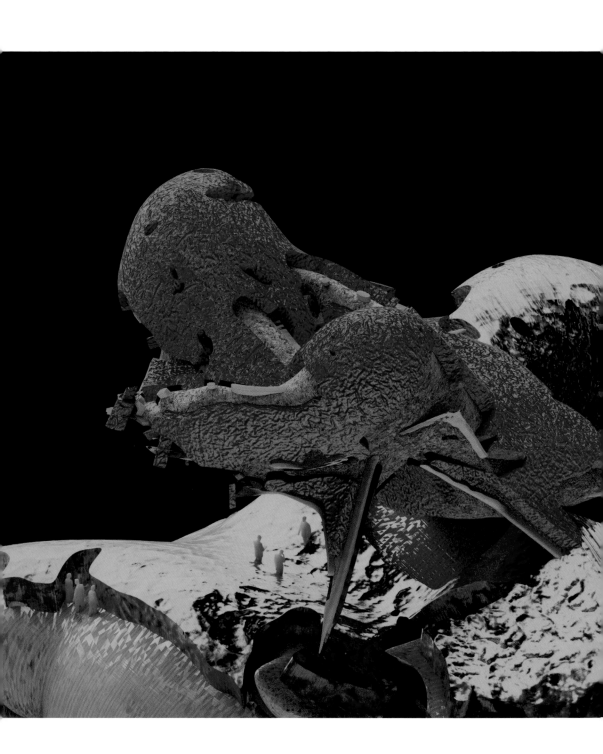

THE FLOOR IS TECHNOLOGY. In a moment of emergent discoveries, how dare architects even consider to disregard technology for progress? Architecture cannot be architecture within the typical notion of itself. Without thinking beyond basic concepts such as framed axial alignment, we shall never reach beyond repetitive ordered design moves. It is irresponsible to declare yourself better by utilizing current, trendy, motifs in architecture, and ignoring what is undoubtedly important. To rediscover classical antiquity, technology is imperative – not only has it changed the way we deliver projects, it has also altered how we think about them. If we begin to re-evaluate key precedents through the lens of our newly emergent technological eye we should be able to extract key new architectural motives. OOO has brought a new level of understanding, when thinking about and consider work – a flat ontological outlook is often key. Know your history. Uncover a future from it. Do not revel in a sea of pastiche.

A FETISH LIKE NO OTHER. Is architecture in a losing battle with machines? We appreciate architecture as an embodiment of machine vision, machine integration and machine thinking as a means to navigate toward architectural progress. Despite this, one wonders – with all emphasis on machines – are we ultimately sidelining architecture to fetishize machine articulation? In many cases yes, we are. We appreciate more the literal translation of machine to architecture through articulations of machine-driven aesthetics, and often the machines that inhabit space are more definable than the architecture. In these cases our architecture acts as a backdrop. This is not something we condone. We must be aware of the battles architecture has previously come across in the form of engineering. We must not allow architecture to become a showroom. We must not allow architecture to lose a battle, which can undeniably be won. For architecture's sake it must be won. Without winning this battle, architecture will rely on the innovations of its past whilst showcasing the future as an object within.

KNOW LESS, THINK MORE. Is it possible that humanity has *learnt* so much that it is hard to believe in traditional philosophical reasoning? We tend to speak through explanations. *OOO – Object-Oriented Ontology* – gives us the opportunity to create (not produce) in the name of design. In the name of aesthetics. In the name of discovery not simply through rational procedural reasoning. We want to find, then cross, the line where philosophy ends and architecture begins. We must look beyond this realm of procedural reasoning – where we must justify every move, every formal decision, through means of programmatic or functional definitions. OOO does not adhere to a style or an array of aesthetics. This may be its downfall, its architectural crux as anything can and anything will be discussed through OOO. Although, we would argue that architecture does not obtain importance by attributing delineable aesthetics. Importance can be found beyond the efficient gradated distribution of program and our utilization of every m². Its influence beyond itself is where its importance will be found.

CONCEPTUAL VANDALISM.
How can we liberate formal mechanisms? A disciplinary focus on location-lodged development procedures will inhibit our ability to design. Intellectual fortifications should not excuse formal shortcomings. We do not propose a banal reductivist look at architecture through appearance, but rather a renewed focus on the Renaissance link between philosophical discussions and architectural formal attributes – Alberti with Grasshopper and Michelangelo with Zbrush.

I WANT TO BREAK FREE. How can architecture affect change? Today's society implicitly teaches the disenfranchised to accept the status quo, with dissent trivialized by the media and platforms of unity or change corrupted by political forces. Architecture has historically been a vanguard to stand against this indifferent reality, which increasingly estranges us from the world and those around us. It is not as simple as offering a luxurious escape from the system (this is in many ways an essential part of its functioning), but rather architecture must offer a real alternative in the form of conceptual and philosophical thought. If we simply design formally or according to commercial intentions we are providing little more than structures of illusion, becoming part of the object we superficially fight against.——28

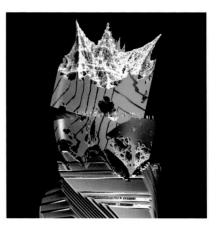

Obj. 238–240

28

Sociologist George Ritzer writes about the 'McDonaldization' of society, which describes society's increasing adoption of the popular US fast-food franchise's characteristics including a focus on efficiency, quantifiability, predictability and control. It leads to a homogenization of culture and a reliance on systems leading to dehumanization.

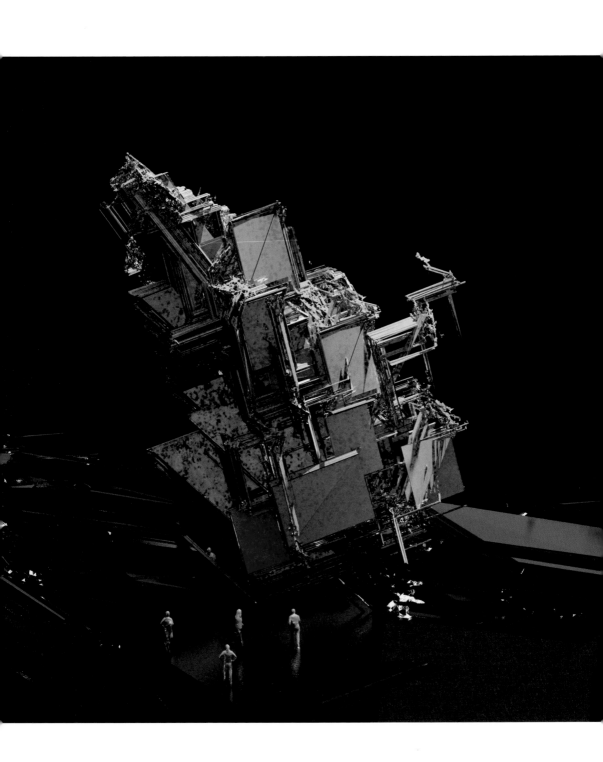

(K)WINTER IS COMING. Can all instances of the *Possible* be realized? The Possible presents a pre-existing image of The Real, but the way in which we may achieve that *Real* must be fundamentally questioned within the context of *Realization* or *Creation.*[29] The first implies a condensed outcome of programmatic reproduction of what has already been tried and tested – with drawings given in advance. The latter promotes evolutionary invention, discovery through the symbiosis of adaptive trial and error, learning from mutation whilst transmitting dynamic forces. Technology has recently given us the capabilities to construct dynamic architecture, which simply do not rely upon given translated data such as plans and sections. With this possibility in mind, we must depart from tried and tested nuances within design and instead seek objects, which traverse new notions of thinking. Embracing architecture, which is inadvertently affected by time in a creative sense and not through construction defects.

UNIVERSALIZED AESTHETICS. Do you feel obliged to please everyone? The misuse and distortion of applications in order to develop forms, textures and strange products of architectural exploration are highly discouraged in many traditional avenues of architectural academia. It is overlooked in practice due to financial adversity. Therefore, our cities tend to look so alike, bordering the pastiche in many cases. By complying with a *universalized aesthetic,* we give up our past, present and our possibly prosperously manifold future. We forget that architecture is not simply an off-the-shelf product like a 40" television, we unambiguously neglect to take into account the impact architecture has but often refer to the Pantheon as *the most influential building of Ancient Rome.* Will your catalogue architectural icon be the most influential building of the 21st Century? We hope not.

———29
Sanford Kwinter distinguishes the virtual from the actual in *Architectures of Time* writing "The relationship of the virtual to the actual is not one of resemblance, but rather of difference, innovation, and creation."

BORROWING SPACE. Does architecture have a reason to exist? An Architectural Object does not charge by the square meter nor promote itself on social media (yet) – but we as the observers, the creators and the investors choose to react in predictable pragmatic ways with an Architectural Object, and that need not be the case. New mechanisms of funding and a speculative temporal view (think blood over money) can run alongside disruptive tech changes – this is the process of empowering architects to *renegotiate* our traditional relationship with financing – fundamentally altering the Capitalist predicament we face. The result has potential to evoke essences, architecture sensations, perceptions and concepts, which are often lost in the distinction between theory and practice. ──── 30

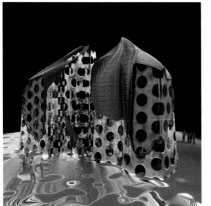

ARCHITECTURE VS. DESIGN. Why are architecture competition juries often devoid of architects? As we design for different stakeholder groups, our sensibilities inherently change. We begin to subvert moments of poetic posture for structural simplicity, ultimately justified through shaving costs, yet we argue and attempt to architecturalize absurdities like the Bilbao effect. We find ourselves claiming to capitalize on this with each and every entry, as though it is a preset command in our CAD software. Our discipline is often seen as a series of building relationships rather than counter-intuitive ideas. Architects as a whole aren't doing much to correct this characterization, especially through our banal, repetitive forms, and our repetitive formal representation (we can't all use *Skalgubbar*).

MOVEMENT IN ARCHITECTURE. What happens when a static Architectural Object becomes infused with dynamics? *Greg Lynn*, once noted that *architecture was the last refuge for members of the flat earth club* – a shame when we consider not only the vitality which movement gives, but also the disconnect such a distinction embodies between us and architecture. New technologies allow new literal and phenomenal understandings of movement.

Obj. 243–245

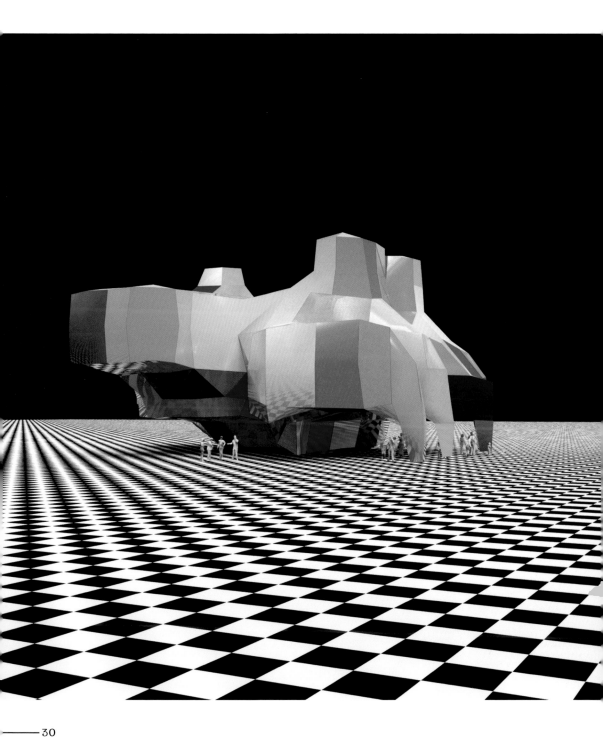

Christo and Jeanne-Claude's artistic works are a great refer-
ence of this new approach. They
create joy through evoking new
readings of familiar spaces,
and their works often confront

the predictability and banality
of our daily routine.

Obj. 246

TRAVERSE. How do architects engage with travel? Not so long ago, the only way to appreciate architecture was to visit it. More often than not, architectural voyages to *distant lands* brought new motivated influence. Today, we find ourselves experiencing the inverse: we may appreciate architecture, augmented and virtually through the 1,038,888 #sagradafamilia tags. Our access to architecture has become so readily available that we've actually reached a point of severe oversaturation. Digital accessibility is undeniably an incredibly freeing thing, however, we must reflect on the intricacies of architecture, which will ultimately be disproportionately undervalued through digital experiences. Architecture in its built form, investigated through physical navigation will reopen a depth to architecture, which is in the process of being partially forgotten.

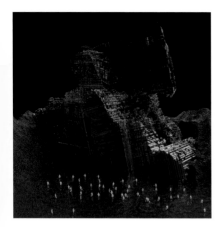

RE:INVENTION. Are we ready for another period of radical architecture? May 1968. This period spurred on an enigmatic, politically charged student force wanting to utilize architecture beyond the physical realm and pursue its abilities to condemn, to comment and to parody the socio-political environment they found themselves within. Are we ready for another round? Generation Y + Z have no collective project as of yet. Instead, we find ourselves fighting multiple socio-political battles on multiple fronts. Our architecture represents a fragmented framework of rebellion, no longer is there a single movement or attitude instead – multiple factions fight smaller battles on conceptual, theoretical and social fronts in order to confront these issues before they become an overarching generational project.

OFFLINE: A NEW LUXURY. Will we ever be alone again? We live in a world where everything is recorded, collected, monitored and stored. A day without your phone is almost unimaginable. There is so much pressure in being *connected*, that being off the grid becomes an unaffordable luxury. There are less and less sacred unmonitored spaces *(white spots)*. The urban setting desperately needs spaces of digital seclusion, and we, as architects, have the power to propose solutions where a series of objects bring that needed balance to the city. Objects in which you cannot check your Instagram. Where nothing is surveyed. Where you are invisible. Where we are invisible. These spaces will let people stop, bringing peace. A moment to think. To recharge for another round of *modern* society.

FLATNESS. Why are symptoms of amnesia productive? In our hyper-stimulated world, there is an increasing need to tell multiple stories simultaneously, each competing for our attention. As a result, a collection of fragments, which we understand have the potential to become greater than their original *whole*. In architecture this idea is supported through concepts like estrangement, a focus on the ephemeral and episodic narratives (like this). As users of architecture, these moments allow our consciousness to reset, refocus and recompose the world around us.

ECHO. So What? The sound of our voice in early telephones used to be different – to our humiliation a simple apparatus changed how we were perceived. What is worse not everyone was even aware of the devastation this

ARCHITECTURE ONTIC. What is the result of a technology-driven aesthetic? Heidegger's *Phenomenological Interpretation of Art* suggests it should create transcendence from within and is tied to an understanding of time and place for a particular person. Such ontological notions may once again find their way into current discourse through Object-Oriented Ontology (though not from an anthropocentric point of view). While traditional art holds cult-inspired aura – human sacrifice – modern Architectural Objects are stripped of human interaction through technological and digital augmentation from within a design and production process. Under the premise of a flat ontology, such *objects* communicate a new sense of democratic power – become *objects* – which expose us as humans to a new world order thereby potentially immunizing us against mass psychosis or radically initiating us into it.

caused to their loved ones. We believe we are the masters of our senses, and yet we don't fully perceive the floor beneath our feet or the air we breathe. Every second we are confronted by layers of meaning by the Architectural Objects we create, and we must embrace what we cannot perceive. Let us celebrate the '*vacuous actuality*' constituted through Alfred Whitehead and try not to rationalize everything into a descriptive list. ——31

Obj. 250-251

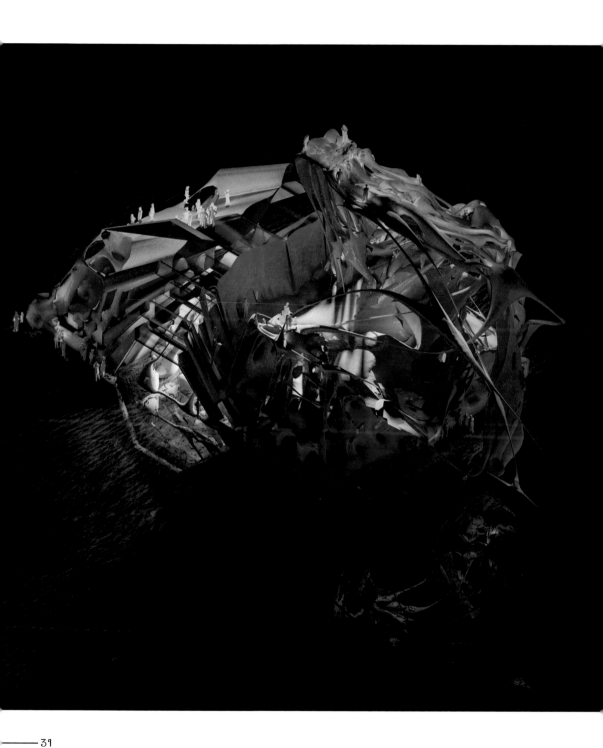

Alfred North Whitehead's metaphysical position in *Process
and Reality* is a repudiation of
'vacuous actuality,' which is
actuality 'void of subjective experience.' An idea that challenges
the correlation between the actual and the factual, and explores
the dichotomy of fact and value.

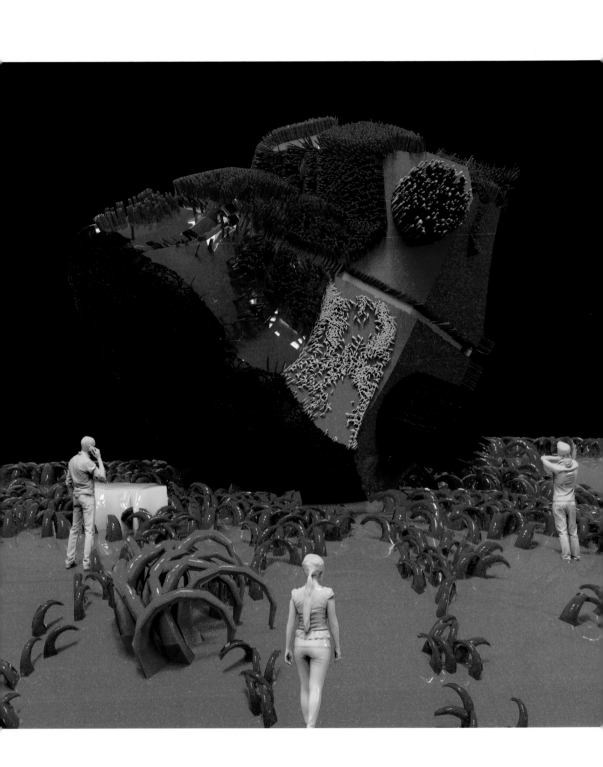

BANAL UTOPIA. Should striving for utopia be humanity's guiding philosophy? Utopia is the ultimate philosophy, the best life attainable. Visionary thinkers have dreamt of structured societies, systematic governments without flaws or questions of failure. A place where regulated rules and orders within society achieve a *utopian* version of life. With these notions in mind, one would question the core values of such an ordered divisive system and quite possibly question the role utopia plays within society. An *ideal* society, and an *ideal* built environment will never mean *utopia* for everyone. Each and every one of us has our own definition of utopia. Therefore we must work on reaching a new normal of the *ideal* where everyone may live in their own version of their own paradise. We prefer clumsy to graceful. Reaching perfection through trial and error. Avoiding rigid rules and procedures. The accidental will allow room to breathe and interpret, which would serve its Utopian purpose to the world.

TOXIC. Is architecture toxic? Sadly it seems, in the eyes of the public, that architecture stands cloaked in elusive ego and power; it is simply misunderstood in every aspect. With the hope of not distancing ourselves from our primary user, we must enable ourselves with language, human relation skill sets and decorum to address architecture for the public eye. Architecture must not become toxic. It must not be an esoteric beacon of ego. Instead our skills must be attributed toward advancing as well as developing the betterment of human existence through unique spatial experiences that can be explored. It must be accessible to all. It must be accessible at multiple levels.

APPROPRIATION. How does the Social Justice Warrior notion of appropriation affect architecture within our objectival context of pastiche, plagiarism, replication and cultural fandom. Considering fascination with: France, Britain, Austria, Pirelli tires, teapots and copper coins an invigorating architectural movement of the weird erupts. The presumably unknown levels of estrangement evoked by an architecture void of all original meaning, void of context conjures a being that itself feels strangely fresh, despite its theoretical age – Postmodernism. The eclectic nature of consumed and regurgitated Architectural Objects evokes the bizarre for those who know, and for those that don't: a critically distant authenticity ensues. Within the very notion of weirdness, we can fundamentally question true cultural meaning within architecture.

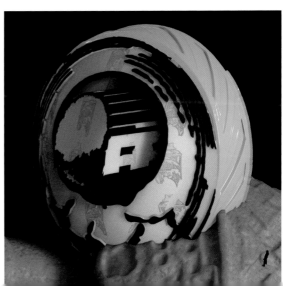

A FAMILIAR FACE. How can we embrace the familiar in favor of the unfamiliar? The epitome of the American home (dream) has been embodied through white picket fencing. Through these motifs of the familiar, any short movements or distortions may tell a story untold, the most subtle movements can have the most important impacts. The movement of a column, shift of a wall, or the melting of a veranda become the most compelling. It's important to acknowledge that these moments seem clear yet become *unfamiliarly familiar* upon closer inspection and thereby derive architectural estrangement. Where the familiar becomes twisted, distorted and fabricated for effect. Those uncomfortable with this are the most altered. We must take pride in these *familiar* mutations; embracing the familiar will encourage the controlled utilization of the unfamiliar.

BANANA GUARD. Are we special? Ontologically speaking we believe that Architectural Objects equally exist. Small/large, complex/simple, replicant/human, the objects around us are equal in being. However, this does not suggest that certain interactions are not preferable to others (from an anthropocentric point of view). OOO can often be confused with Marxist ideas of *commodity fetishism* or tenets of *post-humanism*. While in fact it is a world view which enables us as architects a new-found freedom to pursue non-anthropocentric design ideas in fields such as surrealism, thermodynamics or even within post-structuralism.

STRIPPED BARE. Should Architectural Objects truly be stripped bare like the Modernist legacy we're so firmly rooted in? Louis Sullivan's *Guaranty Building* stands as a terracotta token of decorative, ornamental beauty, defying all Architectural Objects who have been stripped bare. Our Architectural Objects are articulate in their demeanor, empowered by their bump maps and aggressive anti-UV based texture mapping. Ornamentation has changed, augmented reality allows Villa Savoye to wear its own flamboyance and articulate its Pride. No longer must it lay bare in the park. Digital ornamentation will become common ground. One envisions OMA's CCTV HQ in its orange jumpsuit and the Seagram Building sporting a fitting pink tutu. We do not believe Architectural Objects should be stripped bare. They won't be stripped in their physical manifestation and certainly not through their digital transcendence.

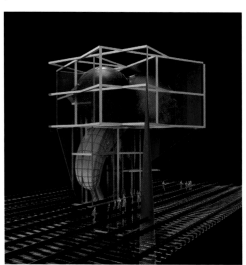

Obj. 255—257

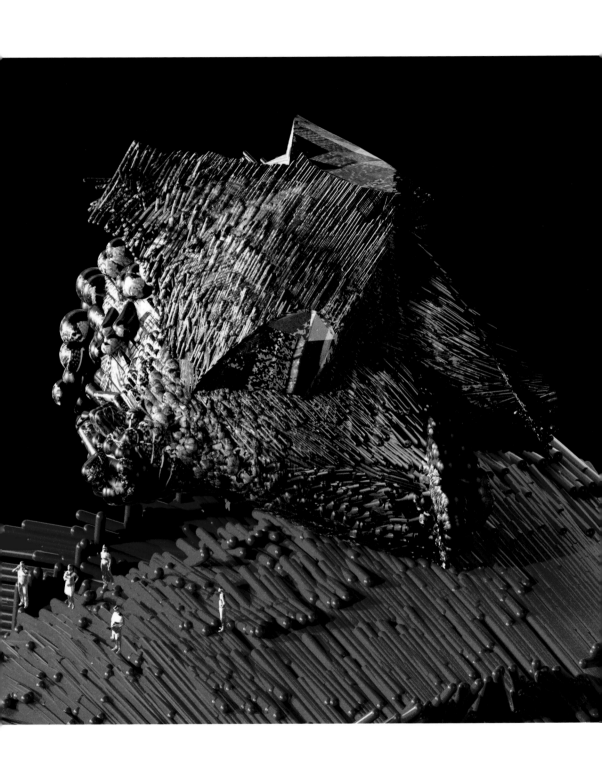

EN PLEIN AIR. Do we follow its principle in architecture? When a person paints a landscape, he tries to depict what's already there; a lifeless copy of life. *Russian Suprematism* suggested that we should think in the perspective of shape and color. At certain moments we need to forget all defined rules and restrictions of our physical reality – as well as our disciplines – and use our subconscious to think purely in forms with pure emotion. Architecture must not be a depiction – a representation, a rendition – especially not a rendition of rules and regulation. It must be an embodiment of our inner most explorative selves.

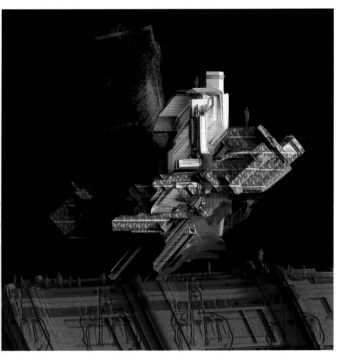

THE ANARCHIST. Through the means of an object-oriented anarchy might we redefine the purpose, or meaning, of architecture? Architecture, in the traditional sense, appears at odds with anarchy. Architecture thrives on corporate polygamy. The city – its love child. May we disarm the city, preventing the construction of an object(ive) fallacy. Instead, we embrace the discontent, deny corporate interference, take control of life and endure the bizarre in favor of freedom. Reject our current acceptance of the city. Burn our modernist *utopias* to the ground. Free ourselves from our corporate overlords. By disconnecting ourselves from this corporate/political control, we will allow ourselves the freedom of expression – as we participate in the 'communal experience.'

I SEE YOU. Should we still concern ourselves with physical presence? One will describe an Architectural Object through what it is made of (construction materials, furniture), another through what it does (brings people together, culturally explorative, hosts events). It is important not to confuse an onto-logical status with a description of internal and external physical environments. Harman claims an Object, is something in-between these two phases. Architectural Objects can exist inde-pendent of its qualities, withdrawn from its rela-tionships and enhanced by its own internalized character-istics.[32] Our aim as ar-chitects is to create objects that exist beyond their rela-tionality, wherein their importance does not come from a lack or abundance of contextual relationships but from themselves as freestanding beings within a contextual vacuum – this reality fun-damentally allows archi-tecture to reassert itself conceptually and physically.

WARNING, YOUR BUILDING HAS CAUGHT A VIRUS! How do we protect our future habitats from obnoxious hackers? The evolution of digital culture has developed a new territory of thinking within architec-ture – regularly we regard it as a machine but not by Le Corbusier's standards. An architecture embedded with technology and digital pro-grams manage our whole spatial experience from con-trolled temperatures to enig-matic lighting conditions. A key concern for architecture consumed by technology is privacy and protection. Our architecture must be cryptic, enabled to defend itself as an autonomous being, which ultimately may be susceptible to digital infiltration. It is im-perative that architects are aware of the challenges and the importance securing our privacy and our shelter through creative autonomous models will bring the future of space.

START OVER. If a person, blind from birth, could have been shown architecture – would they know it is architecture? Architectural academia encourages students to learn through precedent analysis – learning from what has already been tried and tested. Though students confine themselves to churning out, *successful* yet safe buildings; not *architecture*. Borrowing – *stealing* – is common within creative academia. How-ever it rarely contributes anything to-ward discourse. People have presumptuous aesthetics of how objects must look, we must break down these preconceptions. The architectural industry as it stands is based on what has been; it's referential to contex-tual politeness within a cage of historical obedience. Architects are so focused on keeping up architectures tired identifiable brand that they often miss new oppor-tunities to discover or encourage identity within emerging or growing cities. Each and every Architectural Object deserves to have its own integrity instead of a pre-tentious historically contextual guise allowing a building to claim that it is architecture. Let's reflect on history; not simply repeat it.

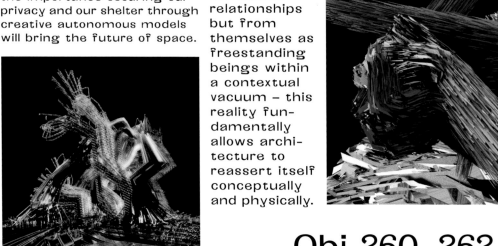

Obj. 260–262

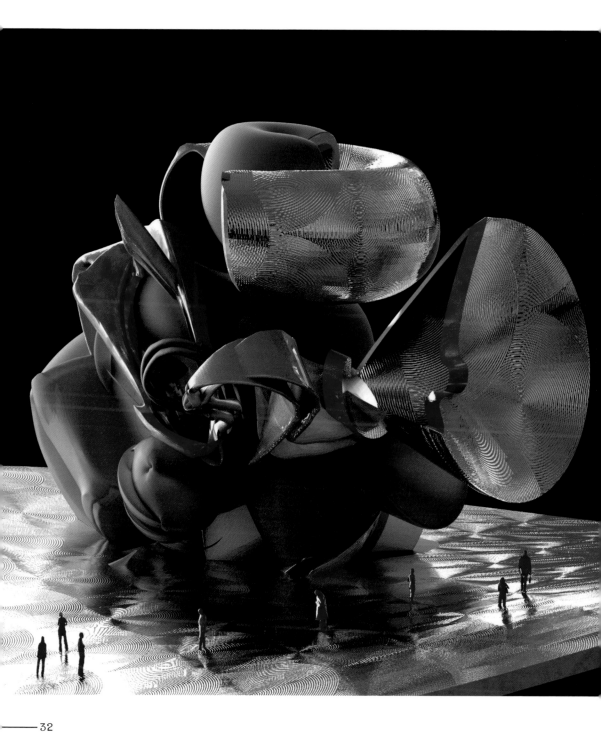

Graham Harman holds that there are two principal strategies for devaluing the philosophical importance of objects. First, one can *undermine* objects by claiming that they are an effect or manifestation of a deeper, underlying substance or force. Second, one can *overmine* objects by either an idealism which holds that there is nothing beneath what appears in the mind or by positing no independent reality outside of language, discourse or power.

Obj. 263—265

TV NOISE. How may architecture address the tatters of our society, our world – in the hope of unity? Architecture has always pushed the boundaries of its profession, nudging at what seems to be defined in order to allow questioning within the fundamentals. Seeping out from a construction nightmare, architecture relishes in the Arts, Philosophy, Science, History and Politics. We aim to fulfill the needs of our disciples, and more importantly the public. Architecture truly stands as a unifying and dissecting means of power. Though it is undeniably tied to financiers who enable it, it lives through means of community and activism – visually, virtually and philosophically. Many influential moments in architecture exist only in the form of a drawing or thought – Étienne-Louis Boullée, Cénotaphe à Newton. Architecture will continue to alter our world as we know it, and as we will know it. However, not through the specificity of policy but through the exploration and contribution of ideas as a collective whole, wherein all may like, share and subscribe.

SIZE MATTERS. Does it really? Norman's phallic presence invades our cities – at every corner. Phallicism in architecture does not view itself as problematic, ridiculous or hilarious, although, it is a mixture of all three. Architects and educators often point fingers at those expressing ego, or those whose work is uniquely distinguished. Yet this ego itself stems from our profession's oppressive gender situation – architecture confined within this framework is problematic. With clients, architects and investors shaking their dicks, asking *whose is biggest?* Architecture finds itself faced with a moral dilemma. Objects are born to find themselves in a *man's world*. It does not bode well for females who may view the profession, both formally and politically, as a vulgar display of pseudo-masculinity. We allow our cities to be penetrated by phallic objects, yet oppose strong feminine presence... *It's much too vaginal.* We must oppose these misogynistic notions of 'fully assumed virility' as Jean Nouvel may put it. We must vie for an architecture, which embraces a diversity of sexuality, gender and understands the multiplicity of political aptitude. Architecture will find fruitful exploration in a world which is ever changing from the non-binary: large, small, camp, phallic, vaginal, to a world not so simplistic in its social understanding and even in its form.

WASHING MACHINE. Can architecture benefit from our impending feedback loop? The cycle of architecture is undeniable in our Modernist tenure. Since the torch has been passed, and modernism has taken shape, the articulation of style, form and repetition comes at wildfire pace. We are stuck in a feedback loop of copies from ripped off Corb and pastiche Mies – the once vanguard have become the new normal. Everything becomes a totalizing moment, an architecture we're all engaged with, an architecture we're all part of. Sadly, this vision ensures an architecture of singular inflections of fantasia with the speed of mass so that the essence of the work is long forgotten. Where is the exit? Taking ownership of this feedback loop will allow us to exploit the lasting moments of excitement buried beneath pastiche idealism. Step aside from poor copies and move towards an enigmatic architecture.

ABORIGINALITY. Do Architectural Objects interpret cultural identity? The traditional semiotic notion of ideological abstraction, as a form of representation, is largely semantically incomplete and often incomprehensible (save for an elite few) – especially when it comes to place-making. While we champion an Architectural Object's ability to create new spaces of cultural significance through their very occupation and physicality (e.g. Gehry's Guggenheim). An avoidance of iconoclastic representation can further the view of culture as an omnipresent subject – rather than a singular object. Similar to Kantian ethical dogma,[33] an Architectural Object must rely on its knowledge of the present to situate itself in the right way, rather than engage in a series of esoteric what-if/parametric scenarios.

OBLIGATORY. How do we address objects of our own inception? Most architecture today consists of deterritorialized objects: withdrawn from social relations, born into a global *internet culture* full of hyperrealism, pseudo-scientific justification and misunderstood plasmatic potential. In this overwhelming context we tend to simplify our designs to descriptions of their component pieces and/or the effects they have within a context, function, performance, a theatre, etc. This simplification is often bolstered by a Maurice Merleau-Ponty-esque visual categorization, which attempts to sell our work within a consumer market. It is time we stop relying on literally descriptive justifications, self-explanatory diagrams, and instead embrace that some qualities are best left unexplained. Let the Architectural Object speak for itself!

Obj. 266–267

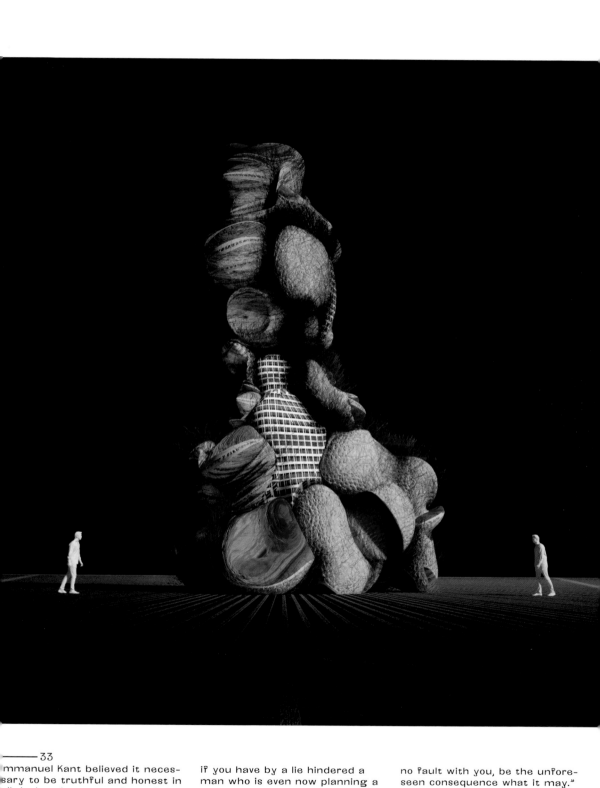

Immanuel Kant believed it necessary to be truthful and honest in all declarations regardless of the situation. In *On a Supposed Right to Tell Lies from Benevolent Motives*, Kant writes: "For instance, if you have by a lie hindered a man who is even now planning a murder, you are legally responsible for all the consequences. But if you have strictly adhered to the truth, public justice can find no fault with you, be the unforeseen consequence what it may."

UI/UX. What is architecture's new digital interface? As our lives become increasingly filtered by digital screens, and we are forced to address the ever-changing physical roles in design. Architectural Objects are evolving, ontological beings going through the same physical/digital crisis. While tools like AR and VR serve as conduits for a new means of communication and interaction, we have yet to embrace these digital mediums as design tools over simply representational techniques. Architecture must embrace its UI and UX to an experience beyond the physical wherein space becomes multi-dimensional and not simply a means to glorify the superficial.

BETWEEN CREATOR AND CREATION. What if architecture can never be truly understood? Žižek jokes that perhaps God was simply a lazy computer game programmer who left parts of our reality unfinished. Akin to the inside of a building you are not meant to enter – assuming we as humans would never be smart enough to investigate the depths of our reality, for example: beyond the atom. If reality is imperfect, then not only is Kant's *finitude* insurmountable, but the same can be applied to architecture via the collision of objects (human and non). This quite possibly suggests that Architectural Objects (AOs) interact in indirect ways. Rather than through seamless gradated transitions, AO interactions are incomprehensibly fragmented and incomputable – without pattern or relationships. As architects we should be cautious of giving meaning based on anthropocentrically read correspondence both physically or phenomenologically.

NON-NON-LINEAR. Are we trapped? Architecture's orthographic foundations once created strong linear ties to striated systems of the State, whilst more curvilinear, fluid forms were able to break into moments of creative freedom. Movements of the likes of Deconstructivism and Postmodernism sought to subvert control via formal articulations that today have been dissolved into a parametric-bim world. What's frightening is that new systems of form generation are often so complex that they can create a false sense of freedom. Often parameterized parameters, driven by choice-obsessed designers create this false sense of freedom fundamentally procuring a tyranny of choice. If we as a discipline wish to remain unabashedly creative we must misappropriate and re-appropriate these *tools* to corrupt and control the underlying technological advancements, which will otherwise be used to ensnare us rather than the endless architectural outcomes.

Obj. 268—270

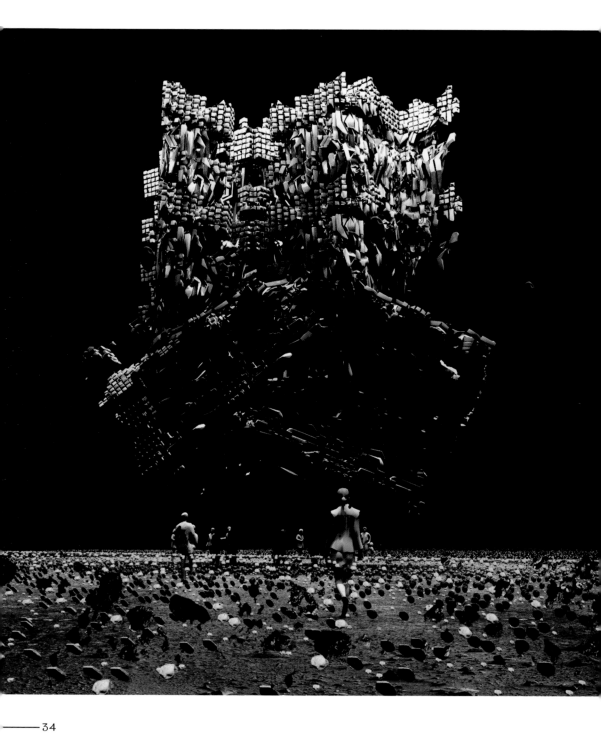

————34

Kantianism is a philosophy of
finitude — because knowledge
and consciousness are not
self-evident; in his work *Critique
of Pure Reason*, Kant relies
on finite beings in order to have

representations and possibility
of knowledge, and thus empirical understanding of the world
around us.

PROPAGANDA TERRAFORMING. In the heat of technology – can we focus on our future and not a future's past? We idolize a 60s notion of the future – the one embodied in futuristic media, even present in NASA's recent *Trappist-1e* poster. This nostalgia no longer has claim to a possible physical existence, it is propaganda that engenders public thought of what the future may look like: we still envision an episode of *The Jetsons*. In reality, these futures depict alternative pipelines to something now unachievable, but their vision and aura has laid down a trail for multi-faceted explorative terraforming. To appreciate this, we need to acknowledge the world's history, its pedagogy and understand the pipeline we are traveling upon in order to further direct our own future.

Obj. 271

BERTH. Where is architecture's allotted place in the universe? Given the current diversification of our profession, architecture can no longer be defined by a series of decisions with the aim of constructing physical objects. Instead, architecture is growing toward a moment of complete integration in our current lives where the edges of building and architecture are blurred with us. Architects now have the capabilities to plan discrete and integrated moments of wonder at micro and macro scale, from pins to planets. Architecture no longer has an allotted position in society, and we already are beginning to face the constant push and pull of other newly formed professions who encroach in our territory as we encroach on theirs.

[DEFECTED] OBJECTS. How might the lives of objects be cherished? *Wabi Sabi* and *Kintsugi* refer to transient worldviews of beauty through imperfection; common shattered objects repaired using finite or precious materials such as Gold. Kintsugi on an urban level gives us the grounding to question the scars, which appear to tarnish our cities and our architectural environment – physically and metaphysically. These scars may bring us enchanted richness, with Architectural Objects applied as the gold which repairs shattered cities. By cherishing and enabling life within an Architectural Object we can emancipate it from a preserved, pristine imprisonment. Each object's growth, its weathered patina, each moment in its existence is work which will never be finished – even in destruction.

Obj. 272—273

AUTHOR BIOGRAPHIES

Aleksandra Belitskaja is an Estonian architectural designer and XR developer whose work centers on novel interactive design models and the interplay of new emergent aesthetics. Her projects focus on utilizing computer graphics and game engine technology to explore new forms of connectivity between audience, architect and community. Her experimental work and proposals have been published internationally. Aleksandra has taught workshops on building dynamic spatial conditions through custom-built game design environments and experimental 3D modeling software. She received her Bachelor of Architecture from the University of Dundee, graduating with distinction, before completing her master studies at the IoA, Die Angewandte in Studio Greg Lynn. Throughout her professional architecture career, Aleksandra has worked for award-winning, internationally-known innovative offices in Stuttgart, Vienna, London and Los Angeles.

Benjamin James is an American-British economist and architectural designer. His works fuses these disciplines by focusing on the use of new disruptive technology in design, specifically, the link between machine vision, machine learning and digital fabrication. Benjamin graduated with honors from the UNC Kenan-Flagler Business School and the Architectural Institute in Prague, before completing his master studies at the IoA, Die Angewandte in Studio Greg Lynn. He has worked professionally on architecture projects in New York, Copenhagen, London and Hong Kong as well as consulted for Fortune 500 companies. As an academic, he served as a visiting researcher at the CIEE Global Institute in Berlin where his work explored computational fluid dynamics and digital fabrication as applied to the architectural discipline. He has been an invited guest at the AA visiting school, in Shenzhen, and lectured in Hong Kong on the impact of new emergent technologies like AR and AI, exploring how they will affect smart cities and New Ruralism.

Shaun McCallum is a Scottish architectural designer and creative technologist whose work investigates the impact of new technologies upon socio-political cultures through ephemeral Architectural Objects and installations. He received his Bachelor of Architecture, with Distinction, from the University of Dundee before studying at the (SCI-Arc) Southern California Institute of Architecture in Los Angeles before completing his masters studies at the IoA, Die Angewandte in Studio Greg Lynn. His projects that explore the accessibility and integration of digital technologies within existing physical structures have received a variety of awards and have been published internationally. As a researcher, Shaun has served as a travel fellow in China investigating the interplay of mystical historical ruins juxtaposed with new consumer-oriented Architectural Objects and under occupied mega cities. With his interests in hybridized realities Shaun has taught workshops on augmented reality and virtual reality through experimental workflows.

iheartblob is an award-winning mixed reality design studio and research collective with a strong focus on the Architectural Object and the role of emerging technologies within architecture. The work is meant to both enchant and reflect on the crisis of thought which runs through architecture today by investigating new and established ideas as though they were materials, engaging seriously with hard-hitting agendas, whilst remaining at a distance from full immersion. The studio has exhibited numerous provocative proposals across the globe including at the Storefront for Art and Architecture in New York City and the A+D Museum in Los Angeles; they have constructed a variety of mixed reality works as physical/digital pavilions for the Toronto Winter Stations Festival and Magazin Gallery in Vienna; and their research has been presented at the Architectural Association visiting school in China and in publications such as Archinect's *Ed* magazine. @iheartblob